Praise for *How to Assess While You Teach Math* . . .

Dana is the rare teacher who sees children as having the right to be a part of the learning process; she believes that young children can and should be involved in their own learning. Step inside *How to Assess While You Teach Math* to see the real power of how formative assessment puts children at the center of learning.

Sheri Willebrand
President, California
Mathematics Council

The word *assessment* comes from the Latin *assidere*, which means "to sit by." *How to Assess While You Teach Math* is an invitation to sit beside and listen to your young mathematicians. Dana starts by suggesting seven must-have practices for formative assessment and then provides integrated lessons that support the practices. She allows us to peek into her classroom as she interviews students, leads whole-group discussions, and uses her interactions with students to inform her teaching. The friendly format, endearing pictures, authentic student work, and Dana's written voice are an incredible combination. I can't decide which I would prefer—the chance for my daughter to be in Dana's kindergarten class or the opportunity to be her teammate at Pueblo Gardens.

Beth Terry
Math specialist, Alexandria
City Public Schools, Virginia;
2004 PAEMST Awardee–Colorado

How to Assess While You Teach Math brings formative assessment into the hands of classroom teachers with easy-to-implement and proven strategies. Using clear and practical approaches, Dana provides educators with the tools they need to uncover student understanding and misconceptions in order to provide purposeful instructional for all learners.

Sherry Parrish
Author of Number Talks: Helping Children Build
Mental Math and Computation Strategies

How to Assess While You Teach Math is a thoughtful and provocative resource focused on how much teachers can enhance the teaching and learning of mathematics by observing, interacting, and listening to children. Dana communicates the power of intentional planning by the teacher so that students can make mathematical discoveries and eventually represent those discoveries with mathematical notation. This valuable resource presents formative assessment as an integral process in getting access to students' emerging mathematical ideas to guide and direct instruction. Respect for the power of students' mathematical thinking permeates throughout.

Olga G. Torres
Presidential Awardee for
Elementary Mathematics

GRADES
K-2

How to Assess While You Teach Math

FORMATIVE ASSESSMENT
PRACTICES AND LESSONS

A Multimedia
Professional Learning
Resource

Dana Islas

Math Solutions
Sausalito, California, USA

Math Solutions
One Harbor Drive, Suite 101
Sausalito, California, USA 94965
www.mathsolutions.com

Islas, Dana.
    How to assess while you teach math : formative assessment practices and lessons : grades K–2 :
a multimedia professional learning resource / Dana Islas.
        p. cm.
    Includes bibliographical references and index.
    Summary: "The lessons in this resource integrate seven key formative assessment practices important to informing instruction: individual assessment, teacher checklists, teacher notebooks, student notebooks, student checklists, student goal setting, and student-led conferences. The accompanying video demonstrates these practices in action with students."
—Provided by publisher.
    ISBN 978-1-935099-17-8 (alk. paper)
    1. Mathematics—Study and teaching (Elementary)—United States—Evaluation.   I. Title.
QA135.6.I75   2011
372.7—dc22   2011001459

The publisher would like to acknowledge adapted material:

page 47: Cubes in a Tube was adapted from *Supporting English Language Learners in Math Class, Grades K–2* (Bresser, Melanese, and Sphar 2008).

page 73: Shake and Spill Combinations was adapted from the lesson Shake and Spill in *About Teaching Mathematics: A K–8 Resource, Third Edition* (Burns 2007).

page 160: The Four-Triangle Problem was adapted from *About Teaching Mathematics: A K–8 Resource, Third Edition* (Burns 2007).

Scholastic is constantly working to lessen the environmental impact of our manufacturing processes. To view our industry-leading paper procurement policy, visit www.scholastic.com/paperpolicy

Editor: Jamie Ann Cross
Production: Melissa L. Inglis-Elliott
Cover and interior design: Susan Barclay/Barclay Design
Composition: Aptara Inc.
Cover and interior images: Pueblo Gardens Elementary School, Tucson Unified School District, Tucson, Arizona, USA
Videographer: Friday's Films, www.fridaysfilms.com

3 4 5 6 7 8 9 10 11 12   31   22 21 20 19 18 17 16 15 14 13

A Message from Math Solutions

We at Math Solutions believe that teaching math well calls for increasing our understanding of the math we teach, seeking deeper insights into how students learn mathematics, and refining our lessons to best promote students' learning.

Math Solutions shares classroom-tested lessons and teaching expertise from our faculty of professional development consultants as well as from other respected math educators. Our publications are part of the nationwide effort we've made since 1984 that now includes

- more than five hundred face-to-face professional development programs each year for teachers and administrators in districts across the country;
- professional development books that span all math topics taught in kindergarten through high school;
- videos for teachers and for parents that show math lessons taught in actual classrooms;
- on-site visits to schools to help refine teaching strategies and assess student learning; and
- free online support, including grade-level lessons, book reviews, inservice information, and district feedback, all in our Math Solutions Online Newsletter.

For information about all of the products and services we have available, please visit our website at *www.mathsolutions.com.* You can also contact us to discuss math professional development needs by calling (800) 868-9092 or by sending an email to *info@mathsolutions.com.*

We're always eager for your feedback and interested in learning about your particular needs. We look forward to hearing from you.

Math Solutions.
FOUNDED BY MARILYN BURNS

SCHOLASTIC

To my husband and my three sweet girls

CONTENTS

Acknowledgments x

Common Core State Standards for Mathematics Correlations xi

Connections to the DVD xiii

☆ SECTION I: HOW TO USE THIS RESOURCE I

Why This Resource? 2

Why These Lessons? 2

How Do I Use This Resource? 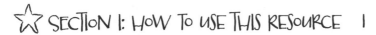 *4*

Three Steps to Getting the Most from This Resource 4

☆ SECTION II: SEVEN MUST-HAVE FORMATIVE ASSESSMENT II
PRACTICES AND HOW TO USE THEM

Formative Assessment Practice 1: Individual Assessments 🔘 *13*

Formative Assessment Practice 2: Teacher Checklists 15

Formative Assessment Practice 3: Teacher Notebooks 17

Formative Assessment Practice 4: Student Notebooks 🔘 *18*

Formative Assessment Practice 5: Student Checklists 🔘 *20*

Formative Assessment Practice 6: Student Goal Setting 🔘 *24*

Formative Assessment Practice 7: Student-Led Conferences 🔘 *26*

Lesson on Setting Goals: The Very Quiet Cricket 🔘 *28*

☆ SECTION III: LESSONS INTEGRATING THE SEVEN FORMATIVE 35
ASSESSMENT PRACTICES

Formative Assessment Through Games 36

G-1 The Attribute Game *38*

G-2 Guess My Pattern *44*

G-3 Building Quantities on a Ten-Frame ⦿ 51

G-4 +1, −1 on a Ten-Frame ⦿ 59

G-5 Practicing Combinations 67

G-6 Shake and Spill Combinations 73

Formative Assessment Through Math and Literature 80

L-1 Ten Black Dots 82

L-2 Five Little Speckled Frogs ⦿ 89

L-3 Color Zoo 97

L-4 The Button Box 104

L-5 Hide and Snake 112

L-6 Lottie's New Beach Towel 119

Formative Assessment Through Problem Solving 126

Looking at Student Work with a Rubric 127

P-1 How Many Frogs? 130

P-2 Combinations of Ants and Grapes 139

P-3 Growth Patterns ⦿ 145

P-4 My Name in Color Tiles! ⦿ 152

P-5 The Four-Triangle Problem 160

P-6 Students Write the Context ⦿ 167

References 207

REPRODUCIBLES

Reproducible A: Teacher Checklist Template

Reproducible B: Student Checklist Template

Reproducible C: Parent Questionnaire

Reproducible D: My Math Goal Is . . .

Reproducible E: Note to Parents

Reproducible F: Shake and Spill Recording Sheet

Reproducible G: Pattern Dance

Reproducible H: Number Cards 1–10

Reproducible I: +1, –1 Cards

Reproducible J: Quick-Image Cards

Reproducible K: The Button Box Recording Sheet

Reproducible L: Lottie's New Beach Towel Recording Sheet

Reproducible M: How Many Frogs? Recording Sheet

Reproducible N: Combinations of Ants Recording Sheet

Reproducible O: Combinations of Grapes Recording Sheet

Reproducible P: Growth Patterns: Comet's Nine Lives Recording Sheet

Reproducible Q: Growth Patterns: Butterflies Recording Sheet

Reproducible R: Students Write the Context Recording Sheet

Reproducible S: Five Little Speckled Frogs Picture Cards

ACKNOWLEDGMENTS

This book has been on my mind for many years; I feel an incredible sense of gratitude as I reflect on the path that led me here. I have been inspired by many rich experiences and blessed to encounter many incredible people along my journey as a teacher. I am truly grateful to Ken Goodman for introducing me to "kid watching," which helped me see how critical this was to making personal connections and academic strides with students. I want to thank all of the dedicated instructors of Tucson Unified School District's Title I/Exxon Mobile Math and Science Project, and especially Connie Lewis for continually pushing me as I learned more about my students and began to refine my craft. She saw potential in me and encouraged me to share my classroom experiences with others, including presenting at NCTM and being part of Math Solutions. I am so appreciative of the opportunities Marilyn Burns has given me to grow as a learner and a teacher of mathematics. I have met amazing teachers from all over the country through my work with Math Solutions. Each one of these teachers has helped deepen my passion for developing an understanding of mathematics in myself and in others.

I want to thank the administration, teachers, students, and parents at Pueblo Gardens Elementary for their support and for stretching my thinking as we engaged in mathematical conversations along the way. I appreciate Debbie Wesch and Enedina Monroy for graciously exchanging students with me. My principal, Marco Ramirez, for creating an environment at our school that encourages teachers to be researchers, continuously learning how to best meet the social, emotional, and academic needs of our students. Through his quest for ways to meet the challenges our students face, he introduced me to Steven Covey's work. I was fortunate to visit "A Leader in Me School" English Estates Elementary in Florida. The administration, teachers, students, and parents of this school embodied what is possible with strong leadership and commitment to a common goal. I thank them for motivating me during my short visit and helping me see how I might connect the loose ends in my own classroom.

I have tremendous respect and gratitude for Sheri Willebrand's knowledge, encouragement, and excitement for mathematics and young children; her insights have helped me shape this resource.

I wish to thank Jamie Cross and Carolyn Felux for helping my vision become a reality. Jamie's talent, gentle guidance, patience, and many poetic emails made the entire process a joyful experience. Carolyn's hands-on support and questioning helped make this resource cohesive.

Many thanks to Perry Pickert and Friday's Films for capturing students' sense of ownership, pride, and perplexity while they enjoy learning math.

My deepest gratitude for my family's incredible, loving support of all of my dreams. Without them, none of my accomplishments would be possible. Julianna's kisses and Isabella's running commentary have been my comic relief. Kirsten's help in my classroom, efforts with housework, and well-timed distractions are always just what I needed! She has enchanted me and my students. Both Kirsten and my sister Dawn Peck have graced this resource with their whimsical drawings. My husband Gregory's cooking and fluency with technology helped me keep my sanity. My parents, Dave and Dianne's love and nurturing care for the girls have allowed me to continue my work in the classroom.

COMMON CORE STATE STANDARDS FOR MATHEMATICS CORRELATIONS

All lessons are correlated to the Common Core Standards when applicable. The correlations are listed with grade (K, 1, or 2) first, followed by the abbreviated domain.

Lesson	Common Core State Standards for Mathematics Domain				
	Counting and Cardinality (CC)	Operations and Algebraic Thinking (OA)	Number and Operations in Base Ten (NBT)	Measurement and Data (MD)	Geometry (G)
G-1 *The Attribute Game*				K.MD	
G-3 *Building Quantities on a Ten-Frame*	K.CC				
G-4 *+1, −1 on a Ten-Frame*	K.CC	K.OA 1.OA			
G-5 *Practicing Combinations*	K.CC	K.OA 1.OA			
G-6 *Shake and Spill Combinations*	K.CC	1.OA		1.MD 2.MD	
L-1 *Ten Black Dots*	K.CC	K.OA 1.OA 2.OA			
L-2 *Five Little Speckled Frogs*	K.CC	K.OA 1.OA			
L-3 *Color Zoo*					K.G 1.G 2.G
L-4 *The Button Box*		1.OA		K.MD	

Lesson	Common Core State Standards for Mathematics Domain				
	Counting and Cardinality (CC)	Operations and Algebraic Thinking (OA)	Number and Operations in Base Ten (NBT)	Measurement and Data (MD)	Geometry (G)
L-6 *Lottie's New Beach Towel*		K.OA 1.OA 2.OA			
P-1 *How Many Frogs?*		K.OA 1.OA 2.OA	2.NBT		
P-2 *Combinations of Ants and Grapes*	K.CC	K.OA 1.OA 2.OA			
P-3 *Growth Patterns*	K.CC	K.OA 1.OA 2.OA			
P-4 *My Name in Color Tiles!*	K.CC	K.OA 1.OA 2.OA			
P-5 *The Four-Triangle Problem*					K.G 1.G 2.G
P-6 *Students Write the Context*		2.OA			

CONNECTIONS TO THE DVD ⊙

The mathematics lessons, assessments, and conferences on the DVD were filmed in kindergarten through grade 2 classrooms at Pueblo Gardens Elementary, a Leader in Me, Covey School, in Tucson, Arizona. All filming was done in May, the final month of the students' school year.

Demographics
The student body at Pueblo Gardens Elementary comprises 2.4 percent Caucasian, 4.1 percent African American, 85.6 percent Hispanic, 3.4 percent Native American, 3.2 percent Asian American, and 1.2 percent Multiracial. English Language Learners comprise 14.7 percent of students. Children who qualify for free or reduced lunch comprise 97 percent of the student body.

Video Clip	Approx. Length	Title and Brief Description	Section and Page Number in Book
Introduction	2:00	*Introduction* Talk with a friend or colleague; what do you see in the introduction that makes you the most excited about *How to Assess While You Teach Math?*	Section I/page 2
A	2:00	*The Importance of Formative Assessment: Insights from the Author* Dana gives brief insights into how and why she uses formative assessment in her classroom. Are some of your practices similar to Dana's? Different?	Section I/page 9
B1 B2 B3	2:00– 3:00 each	*Individual Assessments* Individual assessments are one way in the formative-assessment process to observe and document a student's mathematical understandings. These clips feature three assessments (two counting assessments and one hiding assessment). Are your individual assessments similar to Dana's? Different? How?	Section II/page 13

Video Clip	Approx. Length	Title and Brief Description	Section and Page Number in Book
C	2:00	*Student Notebooks* Kindergartners Carlos and Isabella share the student checklists, academic goals, and personal goals in their student notebooks. What role do you think student notebooks play in the process of formative assessment?	Section II/page 18
D	3:00	*Student Checklists* Student checklists help students record their progress over time. After individual assessments with Yulitza and Taya, Dana shows how to successfully use student checklists. How are student checklists related to assessment data?	Section II/page 20
E	3:00	*Student Goal Setting* Dana describes how student goal setting provides a powerful means of formative assessment and learning in a classroom. Students are seen in action, working on and sharing their goals. How can a student who voices his or her own goal impact the level of family support and involvement he or she receives?	Section II/page 24
F	5:00	*Student-Led Conferences* Kindergarteners Isayah, Michael, and Carlos are all captured sharing their student notebooks with their families. What practices do you use in your classroom to promote student ownership of learning?	Section II/page 26
G	6:00	*Lesson on Setting Goals: The Very Quiet Cricket* Students are seen in action, with *The Very Quiet Cricket* becoming the impetus for generating student interest and excitement in setting their own goals. How would you introduce the concept of goal setting to your students?	Section II/page 28
H	5:00	*Building Quantities on a Ten-Frame* Dana describes the community aspects, benefits, and goals of this game, as well as the types of responses she is interested in seeing from her students. The game is then seen in action on a floor-size ten-frame in Dana's kindergarten classroom. What benefits does a floor-size ten-frame provide students?	Section III/page 54
I	4:00	*+ 1, − 1 on a Ten-Frame* Dana describes how she introduces the game, the goals of the game, and what she looks for as students play the game. The game is then seen in action on a floor-size ten-frame in Dana's classroom. How does Dana use this game to build on student understandings of number concepts?	Section III/page 62

Video Clip	Approx. Length	Title and Brief Description	Section and Page Number in Book
J	7:00	*Five Little Speckled Frogs* Dana describes how her students got hooked on this lesson—and how the mathematical twist encourages students to take the lesson further. The two parts of the lesson are then seen in action in Dana's classroom. How does the use of cubes to represent the frogs give all students access to number concepts?	Section III/page 89
K	5:00	*My Name in Color Tiles!* Kindergartners Michael and Taya show the creative power of this lesson, sharing how their name "masterpieces" became the center of a mathematical task (writing equations that represent the combination of tiles in each letter). Reflect on your teaching practices. How do you support students in strengthening their ability to communicate mathematically?	Section III/page 152
L	9:00	*Growth Patterns* Dana discusses the three critical parts of a problem-solving lesson: introducing, solving, and processing the problem. The clip then focuses on the problem *Comet's Nine Lives* and takes viewers into Dana's classroom for a look at first-graders working together to complete the first two parts of the problem-solving lesson. Reflect on your teaching practices. How do you select problems for your students to solve?	Section III/page 145
M	8:00	*Students Write the Context* Second-graders collaborate on the three parts of a problem-solving lesson (introducing, solving, and processing) as applied to a *Students Write the Context* lesson for the equation $53 - 27$. Reflect on your teaching practices. When and how do you decide which of your students will share their problem-solving strategies?	Section III/page 167

SECTION 1

How to Use This Resource

INTRODUCTION

Featuring video footage from K–2 classrooms, this multimedia resource introduces seven key formative assessment practices, then demonstrates them in action through nineteen engaging lessons. It's the ideal resource for further understanding the *process* of formative assessment in addition to improving your teaching of mathematics. All lessons are aligned to the Common Core State Standards for Mathematics. See the video clip "Introduction" to segue into the DVD. Talk with a friend or colleague; what do you see in the introduction that makes you the most excited about *How to Assess While You Teach Math*?

WHY THIS RESOURCE?

It is my hope that *How to Assess While You Teach Math: Formative Assessment Practices and Lessons, Grades K–2* serves as a practical reference to the strategies and lessons I've found invaluable in helping me further my understanding and use of the *process* of formative assessment—in addition to improving my teaching of mathematics. *How to Assess While You Teach Math* is the multimedia resource I always wished I had—and many educators have requested—in teaching students and mentoring K–2 teachers. It is the culmination of fifteen years of classroom experience, seven years of professional development consulting, twenty years of parenting, and the honor of receiving the Presidential Award for Excellence in Mathematics and Science Teaching—and there's still much to learn.

It's my intention to make your understanding of formative assessment as friendly, practical, and accessible as possible. The lessons in this resource integrate seven key formative assessment practices that I've found crucial to informing my instruction: individual assessments, teacher checklists, teacher notebooks, student notebooks, student checklists, student goal setting, and student-led conferences. In addition, the accompanying video contains authentic classroom footage, giving you the unique opportunity to see these practices in action with my students.

WHY THESE LESSONS?

The lessons in this resource are classroom-tested favorites—ones I have developed over time and know I can count on in informing my instruction. By observing, documenting, and reflecting on students' responses and reactions to these lessons, you will be better able to learn about your students' needs and make the necessary adjustments to their instruction. Each lesson supports implementation of the seven key formative assessment practices.

Finding appropriate lessons can be challenging. During the process of selecting them, I realized that some of my students were struggling with multistep procedures to complete tasks, thus taking attention away from the mathematical emphasis of the task at hand. In these cases, my students were often unable to complete the lesson in a sensible way. The activity the children were working so hard to complete did very little, if anything, to develop mathematical understanding for them; they were simply trying to complete it to please me. Often, students made many mistakes along the way—mistakes they did not even realize. Tasks of this nature do not allow children to begin to think about mathematical concepts. Through formative assessment practices, I was able to reflect on and think about the following situations: What are my students doing? Where are they confused? What is the math I want them to gain an understanding of from this lesson? My goal became to find a way to break down the steps and provide a meaningful context with an emphasis on specific mathematical concepts. It is my hope that the nineteen lessons in this resource will support you in reaching this goal as well.

> *Through formative assessment practices, I was able to reflect on and think about the following situations: What are my students doing? Where are they confused? What is the math I want them to gain an understanding of from this lesson?*

The Importance of Whole-Group Lessons

Many of the lessons in this resource are whole-group lessons. I used to do mostly small-group work, because I felt a small group had more of my attention and that I could learn more about individual students within a small-group structure. Throughout the years, my view has changed; I have discovered many benefits to whole-group lessons. When a lesson is completed by the entire group, it becomes a shared experience that everyone can refer to and everyone in the class has some connection to it. Whole-group lessons provide many opportunities for rich discussions. During whole-group lessons, a larger variety of strategies are likely to be produced and shared, and misunderstandings can be aired and corrected for everyone.

Often, I will put the misunderstanding back out to the students to consider, rather than allow myself to appear to be the person in the classroom with all the solutions. Everyone in the class is part of this community of learners. I am able to learn just as much, if not more, about my students in a whole-group setting; plus, my students are able to learn more from one another!

As I made the shift to teaching lessons in whole-group settings, I had to make decisions about how to monitor my students' participation, their reactions to the lesson, and their mastery of the concepts. Teacher checklists have become an essential tool for me in documenting these important steps. The checklists are a way to organize my observations. I can refer back to these tools to inform my instruction, to look for patterns in understanding or misunderstandings that surface in whole-group lessons. I can also use this information to determine when students need additional support or when they have mastered a concept. For your convenience, every lesson in this resource includes a customized teacher checklist. You can learn more about teacher checklists in Section II (page 15).

The Importance of Student Responsibility

The educational process is not the teacher's sole responsibility. Students and parents must have a vested interest in the outcome, and each must have an active role in the process.

A significant part of formative assessment is student involvement and the ownership a child gains over his or her learning. This is where goal setting, individual assessments, and student checklists come into play. For young children, individual assessments allow a teacher to gain even more insight into a child's thinking and reasoning. This information needs to be documented, and it must also be shared with the child. All students deserve to know what is expected of them and where they fall in meeting those expectations: "This is where you are. What is an achievable goal to work toward based on my expectations and where you are now?"

How Do I Use This Resource?

This resource is meant to be user friendly, practical, and accessible. It is not meant to be the be-all and end-all of formative assessment. It does provide a wealth of valuable classroom-tested ideas that I hope you'll find will enhance your understanding and use of formative assessment. Here is my three-step recommendation for using this resource:

Three Steps to Getting the Most from This Resource

1. Read Section I, "How to Use This Resource." It only takes fifteen minutes to do this. Congratulations! You're already partway there!

2. Read Section II, "Seven Must-Have Formative Assessment Practices and How to Use Them." Watch the corresponding video clips. Familiarize yourself with those practices that are new to you. Comfort yourself with those practices you already know and are using with your students.

3. Dive into one of the lessons in Section III. Once again, take advantage of the video clips—see some of the lessons in action—and the seven formative assessment practices. Come back to the lessons as often as you need to. Do what makes sense to you as a teacher. Understand the mathematical emphasis for each lesson, then tweak the lessons until they make sense to your students.

The following paragraphs provide more details regarding the various parts and structure of this resource.

The Standards Alignment Table

This resource provides a standards alignment table, "Common Core State Standards for Mathematics Correlations" (page xi). It is designed to help make connections between the lessons found in this resource and the Common Core State Standards (these connections are also listed in the opening part of every lesson).

Connections to the DVD

The accompanying video clips are a look at early childhood math experiences. They provide visual guidance for understanding the seven formative assessment practices, implementing the lessons in this resource, and exploring examples of students working independently on meaningful mathematical tasks. Throughout the book, a video icon appears when there is a corresponding video clip. The video clips are organized on the DVD by the corresponding section (Sections I, II, and III) in the book.

The Seven Must-Have Formative Assessment Practices

The seven formative assessment practices featured in this resource have made a significant positive impact on my students' academic success, the role that students play in their own learning, and on my instruction. The practices are interrelated; you will see the best results in your classroom if you use these practices together. Section II explores each practice in depth; Section III offers lessons that support the implementation of these practices. Examples of these practices are also featured in the video clips referenced throughout.

The 19 Lessons

The lessons in this resource are divided into three categories: games, math and literature, and problem solving. The lessons found within the games and math and literature categories are best used to introduce and practice specific math concepts. The problem-solving category contains lessons that provide students with a context to apply concepts and skills they have been learning about and practicing. Last, but not least, Section II contains a lesson on setting goals. Each lesson follows a similar friendly format, as explained here.

Related Lessons

The "Related Lessons" section opens each lesson and is a good place to start. Each section lists suggested lessons to teach before the lesson and/or as a follow-up.

Overview

The "Overview" is a brief introduction to help teachers become familiar with the mathematical focus of the lesson and the mathematical task for the students.

Goals for Student Understanding

This section gives insight into the mathematical concepts and skills embedded within each lesson. The "Goals for Student Understanding" section includes teacher goals and aligns them closely to the mathematical practices in the Common Core State

> The "Goals for Student Understanding" section includes teacher goals and aligns them closely to the mathematical practices in the Common Core State Standards.

Standards. The goals are also correlated with the included teacher and student checklists to help guide your observations of students even further. These documented observations are critical to my next steps as a teacher; the observations inform my instruction. I want to know the following: Have my students gained the mathematical understandings they need from this lesson? Do they need additional experiences and support? Do they need an extension to provide a challenge?

Setting
The "Setting" section suggests the manner in which to group your students during the lesson (whole group, small group, partners, or individuals).

Time
Each lesson lists an approximate amount of time to complete it. Time will vary from class to class, depending on factors such as class size and the time of year the lesson is taught. Procedural tasks—passing out materials, getting to tables to begin working, and so forth—tend to take longer early in the year, before students are accustomed to them. On the other hand, tasks that require students to record their thinking may not take as long early in the year. However, as students become more confident and capable of solving problems in more than one way, they may take more time to record their thinking.

Materials
Each lesson has a "Materials" section that lists the items required for the task. Note that all cards and recording sheets are included as reproducibles at the end of this book. The following is a basic list of materials used in these lessons:

- color tiles
- colored paper (to make precut manipulative shapes of color tiles, pattern blocks, and attribute blocks)
- glue sticks
- interlocking cubes
- masking tape or blue painter's tape (for creating a large ten-frame on the floor)
- pattern blocks
- pencils and crayons
- two-color counters

Key Vocabulary
Vocabulary lists help the teacher identify the terms that can be incorporated and developed throughout the corresponding lesson. Posting key vocabulary for the whole class to see it, before the lesson, serves as a reminder to the teacher and to the students to emphasize new vocabulary before, during, and while concluding the lesson. Some classrooms have a Math Word Wall that includes lists titled "Words Mathematicians Use" or "Words to Describe Our Mathematical Thinking." It is most important to present new vocabulary within a meaningful context. Consider saying the word and asking students to repeat the word with you. I frequently ask questions that encourage the use of new vocabulary. I use processing time to write mathematical vocabulary that the students are using to share their strategies. If the students share a strategy without using the vocabulary I am looking for, I will incorporate it by saying something like, "It sounds like you know you have five on the top

row of your ten-frame since you started with five, then you counted on six, seven, eight on the bottom row. We call this strategy 'counting on.'" Afterward, I write *counting on* where everyone can see it and refer to it as often as possible.

Teaching Directions

Each lesson contains step-by-step directions. Key questions to ask students are highlighted throughout the directions.

Teaching Tips

Throughout the teaching directions of each lesson, you'll find additional short notes based on my experiences with the lesson. These notes are featured as easy-to-find "teaching tips."

Extensions

The "Extension" section of each lesson offers ideas for students who need more of a challenge. The wonderful result of offering an extension in your instruction is that, when some students start facing the challenge, this often catches the attention of others. Those children become interested in what their classmates are working on and want to do the extension, too.

Formative Assessment in Action: Questions

This section in each lesson offers questions to help guide your observations of students as they engage in the lesson. Your focused observations, in turn, support the instructional decisions you make for individual students and your class.

Students Who Struggle

This section describes possible reasons why students might be struggling and offers suggestions for supporting them, including insights on English learners. These suggestions may also be shared with parents to use at home.

What Happens in My Classroom

This section shares, in vignette form, my personal reflections and insights in having used the lesson, as well as any helpful suggestions and formative assessment strategies not covered in the other sections. When possible, these sections include authentic student work from my classroom and/or video footage of the lesson in action in my classroom.

Formative Assessment in Action: Checklists

Each lesson closes with a corresponding teacher checklist and student checklist. These tools emphasize the mathematical concepts being developed within each lesson. The teacher checklist can be used to guide your observations and to record data about your students. The student checklist has child-friendly descriptions of the mathematical ideas in the lesson. It can be used to help children monitor their own learning, set math goals, and share academic progress with their parents. See Section II for more on the use of checklists as a successful formative assessment practice (pages 15 and 20).

The Rubric

In the introduction to the problem-solving lessons, a rubric is included as another way to assess student understanding (see page 128). The rubric helps the teacher determine a way to scaffold the student work for the processing part of each lesson.

THE IMPORTANCE OF FORMATIVE ASSESSMENT: MY STORY

In the heart of a tough neighborhood, Pueblo Gardens Elementary School is a Tucson Unified School District [TUSD] success story, planting hope student by student. We all know that high-quality early education improves the chances for low-income children. And, often, that high-quality early education springs from a priceless resource: a human being. And one such individual is a kindergarten teacher named Dana Islas [emphasis added].
— "Award-Winning Teacher Speaks to Best in Education," *Arizona Daily Star*, January 9, 2010

When formative and summative assessment discussions were just surfacing in my professional world, I had to think of a way to differentiate them in my mind. Here is how I think of the two, in a nutshell:

> *Summative assessment is a summary of what has been learned. Formative assessment is informing teacher instruction.*

As an early childhood teacher, I've always felt a natural affinity toward formative assessment. It has been a part of what I do from the start of my teaching career. My experiences with Ken Goodman at the University of Arizona helped shape the value I place on making observational records. My life in preschool and kindergarten classrooms quickly solidified the need to become a skilled observer of children to document their social, emotional, and academic growth. My ever-morphing organizational skills had me continually gathering data to help make instructional decisions and to write my narratives for each child (there were no report cards for preschool). My need to attend to all the details had me documenting everything ordinary and out of the ordinary.

With more classroom experience, more content knowledge, and a deeper awareness of how children learn, I began using formative assessment more purposefully. Formative assessment gave me the specific information necessary to differentiate instruction and to target individual academic needs. For example, my recordings helped me to see when "out of the ordinary" became a pattern. I found these data necessary and useful in making a case for particular students that I believed to be in need of special services (in some cases, the assessment information I've gathered has led me to realize a student may need more of a challenge than is already being provided). This support may take place as differentiation within a lesson being taught in a small group or individually to reinforce a particular math concept. The additional support may involve me and possibly parents or other family members.

As I learned more about how children learn, I also came to realize how important the role of the student is in his or her academic success. Students need to know what is expected of them and they need information on how to become academically successful. Students can make the decision to be academically successful. Formative assessment includes student involvement. In this resource, in addition to several other essential strategies, I introduce the formative assessment practice of using student checklists. These checklists correspond to each lesson and are intended to help students set goals for themselves. I use these checklists on a continual basis in my classroom; they give my students the opportunity to record their academic success (with my guidance or another adult). The data compiled on the checklist are then referred to when the student writes his or her academic goals. In my classroom, each student keeps his or her checklists and goals in a notebook and they share all this information with their family members at parent conferences. This process allows parents to become aware of their child's goals, the teacher's expectations, what their child has currently mastered, and what they need to continue to work toward academically.

The process of compiling and organizing individual progress has inspired students' desire and ability to become successful more than I could have imagined. I attribute part of this success to the fact that student checklists incorporate a multisensory experience for students. Students hear me talk about the expectations on the checklist (before, during, and after a lesson), then they see the expectations in writing on the checklist. After that, they kinesthetically color the checklist to create a visual to represent their accomplishments. Finally, students describe their checklist to others. This multisensory process has something in it for every student—regardless of his or her developmental stage! (For more on student checklists and student-led conferences, see Section II, pages 20 and 26.)

Student checklists incorporate a multisensory experience for students.

As I continue to learn more, I know I will make adjustments along the way, always with the hope of creating the best possible learning environment for students.

THE IMPORTANCE OF FORMATIVE ASSESSMENT: INSIGHTS FROM THE AUTHOR

CLIP A

In this clip, Dana gives brief insights into how and why she uses formative assessment in her classroom. After watching the clip, think about some of the ways you presently use formative assessment in your classroom. Are some of your practices similar to Dana's? Different? What are you most interested in learning from this resource?

Seven Must-Have Formative Assessment Practices and How to Use Them

This section takes a deeper, albeit practical, look at seven key formative assessment practices that I've found crucial to informing my instruction. Authentic video footage showing these practices in action in my classroom is referenced throughout.

Seven Must-Have Formative Assessment Practices

1. Individual assessments
2. Teacher checklists
3. Teacher notebooks
4. Student notebooks
5. Student goal setting
6. Student checklists
7. Student-led conferences

The seven practices are interrelated; you will find the best results if you are able to use all of them. You may find that you already have some of these practices in place. I am confident that all teachers have assessment data and have conferences with parents. I encourage you to reflect further on how your data are used. How do you organize this information? Who is it shared with? How is it shared? The seven practices highlighted here have helped me use my assessment data in a more meaningful, purposeful way. I am now able to meet the individual needs of my students better while simultaneously empowering them to take control of their individual needs—to take ownership of their learning.

FORMATIVE ASSESSMENT PRACTICE 1: INDIVIDUAL ASSESSMENTS

Individual assessments—meeting one-on-one with a student—are certainly the most direct means of gaining insights into a student's academic abilities and needs. It would likely take a large amount of time, as well numerous sessions while observing students, to gather the same volume of information that can be gathered during an individual assessment. On the other hand, it takes a considerable amount of time to perform individual assessments with each child. It may be difficult to work with one student at a time when the entire class is present. The following are suggestions for how to tackle these challenges and implement individual assessments successfully. Rest assured, the benefits of individual assessments can far outweigh any challenges in administering them!

How Do I Carry Out Individual Assessment During Class?

In my class, I work with students individually when the rest of my students are engaged in independent work. Early during the year, independent work may include the housekeeping center, block center, puzzles, Legos, or computers. As students gain more experience with independent work in the classroom and are engaged in such, I take advantage of this time to work with students individually. Repeated exposure to games and tasks allows for practice and reinforcement of concepts, and gives you (the teacher) the opportunity to conduct individual assessments (as well as use the teacher checklists or work with a small group of students needing additional support). I find it helpful to ask for parent volunteers to come to the classroom to assist students in independent work early during the year.

What Do I Assess During an Individual Assessment?

INDIVIDUAL ASSESSMENTS

VIDEO CLIP B1: INDIVIDUAL COUNTING ASSESSMENT (YULITZA)

VIDEO CLIP B2: INDIVIDUAL COUNTING ASSESSMENT (TAYA)

VIDEO CLIP B3: INDIVIDUAL HIDING ASSESSMENT (TAYA)

Throughout the school year students have a variety of experiences exploring number concepts and relationships. Individual assessments are one way in the formative-assessment process to observe and document a student's mathematical understandings. These three clips show individual assessments with kindergarten students. The first two clips are counting assessments. The third clip shows a hiding assessment.

(continued)

Before watching the clips, consider:
- What are the benefits of individual assessments to a teacher? To a student?

As you watch each clip, consider:
- What do we know about each student's developing understanding of counting?
- What would be the next steps for each student?
- What else would you ask each student?
- (Specific to clip B1) How did the teacher adapt based on what she learned from Yulitza's response, "37, 39, 80" as Yulitza counted the cubes?
- (Specific to clip B3) What information is gained about a student in a hiding assessment?
- (Specific to clips B2 and B3) What do we know about Taya's understanding of number relationships?

After you watch the clips, consider:
- Are your individual assessments similar to Dana's? Different? How?

The types of math concepts I have found to be most successful in addressing during individual assessment are number concepts, including recognizing numbers, writing numbers, counting, understanding combinations, and extending and creating patterns.

Assessing Number Recognition

For number recognition, I list numbers out of order on an $8\frac{1}{2}$-by-11-inch sheet of paper and I ask the student: "What number is this?" This is a skill that, when mastered, will allow students to communicate mathematically much more easily.

Assessing Writing Numbers

Writing numbers is also a skill that enables students to communicate efficiently. For this assessment, I simply ask the student to write numerals in or out of order.

Assessing Counting

During a counting assessment, I observe to find out what quantity the student is able to count to and keep track of. I ask myself questions such as: How does the student do it? Does he or she count the unorganized manipulatives in random order? Slide them to a counted pile? Make a line and then count? Group and then count? And so on. Other questions I may use to guide my observations include the following:

For more questions to help assess students, see the "Formative Assessment in Action: Questions" section of each lesson in Section III.

Does the student know the names of the numbers in order? To what number?

Does the student double-check on his or her own? When asked? Or not at all?

After the amount is counted, does the student conserve? ("So, how many cubes were there?")

Can the student add on? Count back?

Can the student count quantities by twos? Fives? Tens?

Assessing Understanding of Combinations

I've found that the best way to assess a student's understanding of combinations is to use a hiding assessment. For more information on a hiding assessment, see *About Teaching Mathematics: A K–8 Resource* (Burns 2007) and/or *Assessing Math Concepts: Hiding Assessment* (Richardson 2003).

Assessing Understanding of Extending and Creating Patterns

I use a district assessment for patterns. This entails creating an AB pattern with color tiles, then asking students to continue it. I ask students how they knew what to put next. I hide the last three tiles and ask them to tell me the color of the hidden tiles. I do the same thing with an ABC pattern. Finally, I ask students to create their own pattern.

FORMATIVE ASSESSMENT PRACTICE 2: TEACHER CHECKLISTS

Every lesson in this resource includes a teacher checklist. Teacher checklists are invaluable in helping to focus your observations as well as to document student behaviors, responses, and reactions to lessons. I generally use teacher checklists in the form of a table; each column in the table specifies what I'd like to observe while students are engaged in mathematical activities. For example, for the lesson *G-1 The Attribute Game,* one of the columns in the corresponding teacher checklist guides me to note whether and what each student discusses during think-pair-share. (See Figure 1.)

In addition to the observation categories, each teacher checklist provides a column to write each student's name and the date (each checklist accommodates ten students), as well as a column for additional notes and observations.

I get the most use out of a teacher checklist when students revisit the lesson in a setting other than whole group—either individually, with partners, or as a small group. Students proceed to these more intimate settings after they are very familiar with the procedures and expectations of the lesson, and have had ample whole-group experiences with it. This usually ensures that students do not need me to be at their table all the time, giving explanations and support. These settings are also valuable to students, because they gain more time for practice and reinforcement of math concepts previously introduced.

I place the corresponding checklist on a clipboard and circulate, collecting data through my observations. Sometimes students may be engaged in revisiting several related lessons; in such cases, I may have several different checklists on my clipboard. As I circulate, I observe and take note of students' reactions, responses, progress over time, use of vocabulary, and interactions with a partner or group.

I also use teacher checklists to document my observations made during a whole-group setting. This is more challenging for me to accomplish, because my thoughts in whole-group

TEACHER CHECKLIST: THE ATTRIBUTE GAME

Student Names and Date	Participates Only When Asked	Predicts Attribute/Refines Prediction	Discusses During Think-Pair-Share	Categorizes Attributes Have, Have Not	Sorts to Choose Attribute to Be Guessed	Notes
Work of 9/26–9/30						
Andres	✓					listening very quietly
Bella		✓	✓	✓	✓ color	confident; eager to share ideas
Julie		✓	✓	Not consis- tantly		listens first during think pair-share
Sam		Predicts ✓	✓			not refining
Bill		Predicts ✓	✓			
Kirsten		✓	✓			
James		✓	✓	Not consis- tantly		
Aidan		Predicts ✓	✓			
Natalie	✓					excited to come up for others to guess
Ted		✓	✓	✓	✓ stripes	

FIGURE 1 An example of a completed teacher checklist for the lesson G-1 The Attribute Game.

settings are primarily on questioning and keeping the lesson progressing in a meaningful manner. I usually have to record my observations after the whole-group setting. Regardless, having the teacher checklist ready on a clipboard and easily accessible helps ensure that necessary documentation and recording takes place.

Each lesson in this resource has a corresponding teacher checklist. Also included is a blank teacher checklist template (see Reproducible A) for you to modify and/or create your own teacher checklists. After you've completed your checklist, it's important to reflect and review continually the student data. The following are key questions to help guide you further in using teacher checklists as a formative assessment practice:

REPRODUCIBLE A

Key Questions for Guiding Decisions Based on Teacher Checklist Data

What are students successful with?

What concepts have students mastered?

What are the next steps for these students?

What concepts do students need additional support and experience with?

What are the next steps for those students who need additional support?

What goals do I have for each student?

What are reasonable goals for students to set for themselves?

FORMATIVE ASSESSMENT PRACTICE 3: TEACHER NOTEBOOKS

Although the value and need for observing and recording my students' reactions and responses to lessons was clear to me, how to organize it in a useful manner was not. The information I gathered about each student helped me make decisions to meet his or her academic, social, and emotional needs. I used the data for parent–teacher conferences and to write report cards and narratives. Some of my observational records supported referrals I made. My documentation helped make a case for students to receive additional services to support their academic growth. Through all of this, I had tried a variety of recording and organizational strategies, but always fell short of finding a system that I could maintain as well as I wanted or needed to—until I discovered the value of a simple teacher notebook while visiting "A Leader in Me School."

I now keep all of my student data in a large three-ring binder. The information is separated by tabs, which are organized by data type. Types of data in my binder include everything from district forms and photocopied emergency cards to quarterly writing prompts, individual assessments, report cards, and photocopies of dated referrals. Every teacher's binder will likely be different in terms of what makes sense to you to include. The following is a checklist I use for my teacher notebook:

> ### *Teacher Notebook: Student Data to Include*
>
> District forms (dress code policy, media consents, and so on)
>
> Parent questionnaire (I ask parents to complete a questionnaire at the beginning of the school year; see Reproducible C at the end of the book.)
>
> District-required and teacher-created assessment data for all subjects
>
> Teacher checklists
>
> Progress reports
>
> Report cards
>
> Copies of referrals for any services
>
> Blank student checklists (See Reproducible B: Student Checklist Template at the end of the book.)

In the past, I stored all this information in separate file folders in a filing cabinet. By keeping everything all together in one binder, this information is now a living resource. I use the student data in a more reflective, meaningful way, in part because it is more accessible. I can see more easily and quickly the documentation of students' progress over time. I can make comparisons more easily between different assessment tools and across subject areas. This is all a result of the fact that everything is in one place: my teacher notebook. If I need to take student data to a meeting to help make a case for a student to receive services, I already have gathered everything I need. If a parent asks for information about his or her child's progress, I have all my paperwork organized and ready to share. This simple organizational practice is sure to improve instruction and make keeping track of student data easier.

FORMATIVE ASSESSMENT PRACTICE 4: STUDENT NOTEBOOKS

STUDENT NOTEBOOKS
VIDEO CLIP C

This clip shows Carlos and Isabella sharing their student notebooks with their families. They talk about math goals they wrote and accomplishments they made during kindergarten. *As you watch this clip, consider:*

- What role do you think student notebooks play in the process of formative assessment?

- What benefits do student notebooks offer teachers? Students? Parents? Other family members?
- How do student notebooks become the vehicle used to communicate what is valued in a classroom?
- How do student notebooks empower students?

Just as I recommend you have a teacher notebook, each student in my class has his or her own student notebook. These notebooks hold their student checklists, academic goals, and personal goals (this is also a practice I saw during my visit to English Estates Elementary). I use binders that have a clear plastic sleeve as the front cover and a clear sleeve on the spine. I ask each child to create a self-portrait for his or her notebook to personalize it; this self-portrait slides into the front cover sleeve. I type each student's name in a large, bold font and slip these labels into the sleeve on each binder's spine. I store the binders on a shelf that students can readily access.

My students' binders are empty at the beginning of the year. Student checklists and goals are gradually added to each child's binder. After individual assessments, I share feedback with the student; the student uses a crayon or marker to color appropriate sections on his or her corresponding checklist, thus keeping track of his or her progress. Afterward, the checklist is added to the student's notebook. (See Figure 2.) Some students have different checklists in their binders; I modify checklists depending on the student and where he or she is in his mathematical proficiency (for more on student checklists, see page 20). As a class, we also spend time writing academic goals. Each student places his or her goals in their notebook (for more on student goal setting, see page 24).

When I have shared my student notebook practice with others, I have had teachers comment that these notebooks remind them of the portfolios we used to keep on each student. Although I agree that there are similarities, there are some very important differences. Portfolios are a collection of assessments—some required by the school district, some that are teacher created. Artifacts

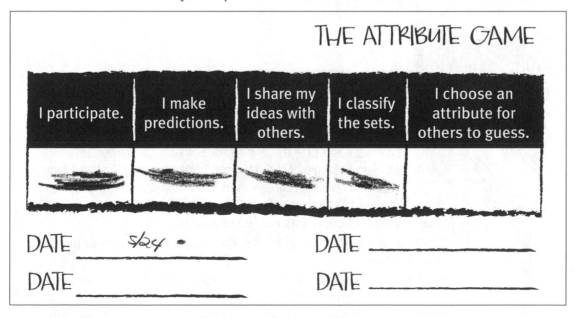

FIGURE 2   An example of a completed student checklist for the lesson G-1 The Attribute Game. This checklist is added to the student's notebook.

of student work are also included in portfolios, often accompanied by anecdotal notes from the teacher. In my classroom, the students completed their work and assessments, and stored the items in their portfolio. The contents of the portfolios were not revisited very often. At the end of the school year, the portfolios were passed on to the next year's teacher to give insight to the student and his or her academic standings.

Student notebooks are a formative assessment practice that directly involves students in charting their academic and personal progress. The teacher completes a variety of formative assessments and the students record their efforts in a color-coded manner on student-friendly checklists. The checklists are revisited regularly to record progress over time (see the next section for more on us-

ing student checklists). Students become aware of their teacher's academic expectations; they also become aware of where they are in relationship to these expectations. Parents and students beam with pride when they see, while reviewing the student's notebook, how much has been learned from one data-recording session to the next. For more information on student notebooks see *The Leader in Me: How Schools and Parents Around the World Are Inspiring Greatness, One Child at a Time* (Covey 2008).

FORMATIVE ASSESSMENT PRACTICE 5: STUDENT CHECKLISTS

STUDENT CHECKLISTS
VIDEO CLIP D

This clip addresses the importance of student checklists. It gives an example of how to record data on a checklist and how a student checklist can be used to summarize progress with a student after an assessment. *As you watch the clip, consider:*

- How are student checklists related to assessment data?
- What is the significance of having the student fill out his or her own checklist?
- How does this recording system make assessment data useful to the teacher? To the student?
- What other checklists would be important for students to include in their student notebooks?

Number Recognition 0-20

0		10		20	
1		11			
2		12			
3		13			
4		14			
5		15			
6		16			
7		17			
8		18			
9		19			

Date 8/28/09   Date 12/1

Date 10/22   Date 5/25

FIGURE 3 Completed Student Checklist:
Number Recognition to 20.

I Can Count! 1-30

1		11		21	
2		12		22	
3		13		23	
4		14		24	
5		15		25	
6		16		26	
7		17		27	
8		18		28	
9		19		29	
10		20		30	

Date 8/28   Date 12/1

Date 10/19   Date

I touch each object as I count._____

I am organized._____

I add on._____

I can count by 2s._____

I double check._____

FIGURE 4 Completed Student Checklist:
Counting to 30.

I Can Count! 1-50

1		11		21		31		41	
2		12		22		32		42	
3		13		23		33		43	
4		14		24		34		44	
5		15		25		35		45	
6		16		26		36		46	
7		17		27		37		47	
8		18		28		38		48	
9		19		29		39		49	
10		20		30		40		50	

Date 12/1   Date

Date 5/20   Date

I touch each object as I count._____

I am organized._____

I add on._____

I can count by 2s._____

I double check._____

FIGURE 5 Completed Student Checklist: Counting to 50.

Templates of these checklists are downloadable from www.mathsolutions.com/howtoassessreproducibles.

BUILDING QUANTITIES ON A TEN-FRAME

I recognize numbers.	I build sets.	I build top, left to right, then bottom, left to right.	I build from the counters already on the ten-frame.
~~	~~~		

DATE _____ 10/26 _____   DATE _____

DATE _____   DATE _____

FIGURE 6 Completed Student Checklist: G-1 Building Quantities on a Ten-Frame.

GUESS MY PATTERN

I recognize a pattern.	I know why it is a pattern.	I can extend a pattern.	I know where the unit repeats.	I can create my own pattern.
~~	~~~	~~~		~~~

DATE _____ 12/9 _____   DATE _____

DATE _____   DATE _____

FIGURE 7 Completed Student Checklist: G-2 Guess My Pattern.

Student checklists include most of the information on a teacher checklist (refer back to Figure 1 for a sample teacher checklist). Student checklists are written simply, in student-friendly language. These checklists help students record their progress over time. Each child should have his or her own student checklist and keep it in his or her student notebook. (See Figures 3 through 7.)

Information can be recorded on a student checklist in several ways. Early during the school year, I may allot colors to each month—for example, green for August, blue for September, orange for October, and so on. I then meet with each student, read the categories across the top of his or her student checklist, and discuss each category with the student to determine whether he or she has met the requirements of the category. If the concept is met, I make a dot—using the color that corresponds to the month we're in—in the corresponding space on the student's checklist. I also model how I expect a child to color in the spaces on his or her checklist. Afterward, I ask the student to color in those spaces that have a dot. I tell the student that the color we are using will remind us that this is what he or she knew in August, for example. If the requirements for the category have not been met, the space is not colored in. Helping children understand why or why not a space is colored in motivates them to make a plan and work toward achieving their goals.

Instead of months, you might have colors designate a particular time period. For example, your first individual assessments might use yellow; your second assessments, purple; and so on. Also, for the first quarter I might use orange, the second quarter I might use green, and so forth. Whatever system you choose to use, make sure you vary colors; color coding makes it easy to compare data over time.

Note that some students have different checklists in their binders; I modify checklists depending on the student and where he or she is in his or her mathematical proficiency. For example, the checklist that records how many objects a student can count is unique to the child. I would not want a student to become overwhelmed with a checklist that has spaces for counting fifty objects when he or she is only able to count five objects accurately. It makes sense for this student to begin with a counting checklist with spaces for counting ten objects. The student feels a sense of accomplishment when he or she can fill in all ten spaces and is able to count ten objects accurately, with the page complete. Imagine how children would feel if they were given a checklist for counting fifty objects. There would still be forty empty spaces staring back at them!

Student checklists should be shared with family members to support teacher and student efforts. This can be done through a conversation with the parent as the student is picked up from school. If you do not see a parent regularly, consider photocopying the student's checklist and writing a message on it to send home with the child.

Student Checklists: A Multisensory Experience

Student checklists provide a multisensory experience for students. In my classroom, students hear me talk about the expectations on the checklist (before, during, and after a lesson), then they see the expectations in writing on the checklist. After that, they kinesthetically color in the checklist to  create a visual to represent their accomplishments. Finally, students describe their checklist to others. This multisensory process has something in it for every student— regardless of his or her developmental stage!

FORMATIVE ASSESSMENT PRACTICE 6: STUDENT GOAL SETTING

STUDENT GOAL SETTING

VIDEO CLIP E

This clip gives an example of how, when students set their own goals, it provides a powerful means of formative assessment and learning in a classroom. *As you watch the clip, consider:*

- What is the significance of students setting academic goals?
- How does the process of a student sharing his or her academic goal make a parent or family member more aware of the teaching and learning taking place in the classroom?
- How can a student who voices his or her own goal impact the level of family support and involvement he or she receives?

A significant part of formative assessment is student involvement and the ownership a child gains over his or her learning. This is where setting goals comes into play. Within the first few weeks of school, I begin to read books to my class that have goal-setting themes; such books encourage each child to set goals for him- or herself (see the goal-setting lesson *The Very Quiet Cricket*, page 28). I want each student to make an achievable plan and I want to support each in reaching his or her goals. At the beginning of the school year, I also work with each child individually to assess what he or she knows. The assessment data help me plan meaningful instruction and help students set goals for themselves. The assessments are useful when students set their goals, because each student and I can refer to what he or she already knows. If a student can count fifteen objects accurately, she should push herself to count to a larger quantity. I remind students of the goals they have set for themselves and make direct connections between the focus of particular lessons and the goals that students have set individually. I also use students' self-set goals to motivate students and keep them on task with what they want to achieve. For example, during a short conference in which I'm recording a student's progress, I might encourage the child to revisit his goals and ask him, "*Building Numbers on a Ten-Frame* and *Popcorn Math* are both games to help you learn more about counting. Which one are you going to play?"

The goals that children write—as well as the assessment data I've collected—are wonderful to share with families at parent–teacher conferences. It is even more powerful when children are present at the conference and are given the opportunity to talk about their goals with their family members. The teacher, student, and parents can revisit the student's written goals to determine whether the goals have been met. Setting new goals may be necessary—and achieved goals are celebrated. In some cases, conversations may take place about what should be done to work toward reaching a particular goal.

For example, one of my students could count four objects successfully in August. Carol was determined to count to one hundred and she wanted to make this her math goal. Going from counting four objects to one hundred objects is a huge jump. I encouraged Carol to set smaller, attainable short-term goals, while keeping in mind that she was on the path to counting one hundred objects. Carol shared her notebook (and her goal) with her parents at a conference in September. She then routinely practiced counting at home and was usually on task throughout the day at school. She worked toward her goal above and beyond my expectations. When I reassessed Carol in late October, she could count to one hundred orally, and successfully count one hundred interlocking cubes. She created sticks as she counted and kept track, and added on all the way to one hundred objects! I was truly impressed, especially with her determination to reach her goal—and the power that setting goals can instill in children.

It's also fair to point out that during Carol's reassessment, I realized she was making very little gains in number recognition. This was surprising to me; we had been focusing on numbers since the beginning of school. Carol was resourceful; she was able to locate numbers within the classroom and determine numeral names as necessary using her strong counting skills. Although we had reason to celebrate Carol's achievement of her goal in counting to one hundred, we also had to focus seriously on her next steps in achieving other goals. After Carol recorded the additional two numerals that she recognized since the earlier assessment in August, I asked her if she thought working toward recognizing all of the numbers between zero and twenty would be a good goal to set. She agreed that it would be. I asked her to help me think of ways to practice at home and at school that could help her work toward her goal. What games might be helpful? We came up with *Number Bingo*, flash cards, writing numbers, and card games. I shared all this news through a short, informal conversation with Carol's dad when he picked her up from school. Carol's dad was thrilled with the news and took her out for pizza for reaching her counting goal. He was also aware of what she needed to focus on for her next goal.

Although all students do not make the same gains as Carol in such a short amount of time, nor have the same amount of determination or support at home, it is important to motivate students and to capitalize on their connections with family members. When my students set goals, I make a point to share their goals and an achievement plan with their family. If I do not see the student's parents, I ask aunts, uncles, older siblings, and other caregivers to practice and reinforce specific skills with the student. I also make sure I have conversations with each student, acknowledging his or her gains and brainstorming new goals. These conversations help students realize the role they play in their own academic success, as well as motivate them to set goals and work toward seeing each goal through to completion.

FORMATIVE ASSESSMENT PRACTICE 7: STUDENT-LED CONFERENCES

STUDENT-LED CONFERENCES
VIDEO CLIP F

This clip shows examples of student-led conferences in which young children take ownership of their learning and communicate their academic goals and progress to family members. *As you watch the clip, consider:*

- How can a student-led conference empower a child?
- How can a student-led conference impact family involvement in attending conferences? In having interest in the child's education? In supporting the child's realization of academic goals and academic progress?

After you watch the clip, consider:

- What practices do you use in your classroom to promote student ownership of learning?

A last, but not certainly not least, recommended formative assessment practice is student-led conferences with parents or family members. While visiting a "Leader in Me School, English Estates," I saw firsthand how student-led conferences promote student ownership of a child's learning. Student-led conferences are a time for children to share their developing sense of ownership of their learning, their self-set goals, and their progress. To set up a student-led conference, I make sure there is a table or adequate space for the student to share his or her notebook, as well as appropriate seating for each family member. I make a point not to be at the table with the student and his or her family; rather, I am physically close by, available to answer parents' questions and support students as needed while they share the contents of their student notebooks. This is each student's time in the spotlight; each child is very proud of the work he or she has accomplished and is excited to guide family members through their student notebook.

> *Student-led conferences are a time for children to share their developing sense of ownership of their learning, their self-set goals, and their progress.*

To prepare for student-led conferences, I first ask my students to share their notebooks with each other. I select partners for each child to sit with. I remind the students that the spaces on their checklists that are colored show what they know, and the spaces that have not been colored show what needs to be practiced. I send a few children at a time to get their notebooks. Each student takes turns sharing his or her goals and student checklists with a partner. After students have shared with the partner I selected for them, they may choose a different partner. I emphasize that, ultimately, students will be sharing with their parents or family members.

Giving students the opportunity to practice student-led conferences helps them become more confident and prepared to share during the actual event. Students build their excitement to tell their parents about their notebooks. In turn, such excitement encourages more families and family members to create time in their busy schedules for the conferences—and for supporting their child's learning. For more information on student-led conferences see *The Leader in Me: How Schools and Parents Around the World Are Inspiring Greatness, One Child at a Time* (Covey 2008).

LESSON ON SETTING GOALS: THE VERY QUIET CRICKET

Related Lessons

This lesson is uniquely related to each of the lessons offered in this resource. It sets a foundation for formative assessment as students begin to take ownership of their own learning.

Overview

This lesson uses the literature piece *The Very Quiet Cricket* by Eric Carle (1990) as the impetus for generating student interest and excitement in setting their own goals. *The Very Quiet Cricket* tells the story of a young cricket with a desire to chirp "Hello" to each of the insects he encounters. In the beginning of the story, he is very small, very young, and unable to chirp. As he grows and continues to practice, he learns to chirp, hence achieving his goal. The lesson helps students think about setting a goal for themselves and practicing to achieve the goal. It can be used to help students write math, become literate, and set personal goals.

Goals for Student Understanding

Students will

- recognize that they each have a role in their own academic success;

- understand that a goal is something that they are unable to do at this time, but it is something to work toward; and

- learn that after their goals are written, a plan needs to be made to work toward each goal— the plan includes the teacher, student, and family members.

Setting

Whole group or small group

Time

Approximately forty-five minutes

Materials

The Very Quiet Cricket by Eric Carle
Reproducible D: My Math Goal Is . . . ,
    1 copy per student
Reproducible E: Note to Parents, 1 copy
    per student

Key Vocabulary

achievable
goal
plan
practice

TEACHING DIRECTIONS

Part 1: Reading the Book

1. Tell students you will be reading the familiar story *The Very Quiet Cricket* by Eric Carle. While you read the story, ask them to think about the answer to the question: What did the cricket want to do that he was not always able to do?

2. Read the story.

3. After reading the story, ask students: What did the cricket want to learn to do? Remind students that the cricket had a goal of learning how to chirp. Ask students: How do you think he learned to chirp by the end of the story? Did the cricket give up when he was unable to chirp?

4. Have students do a think-pair-share. Ask them to think about something each of them learned to do, then share what they learned to do with the person next to them. Then ask a few children to share what they said with the whole group.

Part 2: Setting Goals

5. Explain to students they will each be setting a math goal. Ask them to think of something they would each like to learn to do in math. It must be something they cannot yet do but would like to be able to do.

6. Show students a copy of Reproducible D: My Math Goal Is . . . . Explain that each student will get a copy of this sheet and that they will need to describe their math goal in writing on the lines provided. In the rectangular space, they will need to draw a picture that represents them working on their math goal. Hand out the sheets and have students work independently on their goal. (See Figure 8.)

> **TEACHING TIP: STUDENTS WHO STRUGGLE**
>
> Some students may have difficulty thinking of an appropriate math goal. This is an ideal opportunity to refer each student to his or her student notebook. Ask students: What do you already know? What would be a good next step?

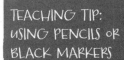

REPRODUCIBLE D

Part 3: Discussing Goals

7. As students finish, ask them to bring their papers to you. Have a short conversation with each child about the goal he or she has written. Ask questions such as the following. Write notes from your conversation on the bottom of each child's paper.

> ***Questions to Ask Each Child About Their Goal***
>
> What are you going to do at school to reach this goal?
>
> What can you do at home to work toward your goal?
>
> Who will work with you at school? At home?

> **TEACHING TIP: USING PENCILS OR BLACK MARKERS**
>
> I usually have students complete their drawings in pencil or in black marker so I can get a clear photocopy of each student's work to share with their families. Crayons and colored markers do not always photocopy well.

Part 4: As Students Finish

8. After each student has finished talking about his or her goal with you, ask them to work at flat pattern block designs or to read a book from the classroom library. Pattern blocks and books offer students a choice within the boundaries you are setting. Both

FIGURE 8 Reproducible D: My Math Goal Is . . .

pattern blocks and books provide engaging, independent work for young children. Having students work independently after they finish writing their goal allows you an opportunity to have individual conversations with students. In addition, pattern blocks and books can be cleaned up quickly after everyone finishes writing and discussing their goals.

Part 5: Sharing Student Goals with Families

9. Photocopy the My Math Goal Is . . . papers. Make sure you include notes on each from your short conferences with each student (see the "Teacher Notes" section of Reproducible A). Send copies home with a "Note to Parents" message attached (see Reproducible E: Note to

Parents). The note to parents has a place for parents to sign to acknowledge receipt of their child's goal and the child's plan to achieve the goal. The original "My Math Goal Is . . ." papers should be placed in each student's notebook by the student.

FORMATIVE ASSESSMENT IN ACTION: QUESTIONS

Ideally, have students write goals within the first month of school (note that even kindergartners can write goals!), and definitely before parent–teacher conferences. Students can then share their goals with their parents during conferences. Goals written and voiced by the child

---

MY MATH GOAL IS

DATE   08/15

MY MATH GOAL IS . . .

to write numbers.

TEACHER NOTES:

FIGURE 9 Janeim's written goal at the beginning of the school year was to write numbers.

MY MATH GOAL IS

DATE   12/10

MY MATH GOAL IS . . .

TEACHER NOTES:

FIGURE 10 Janeim's written midyear goal was *I want to count to 30.*

to his or her parents are much more meaningful. (See Figures 9 through 11.) This formative assessment practice helps parents understand early during the school year that goal setting is part of their child's experience and that they have a role to play in their child's academic success. (See page 24 for more on the formative assessment practice of students setting their own goals.)

MY MATH GOAL IS

DATE   05/03

$$1+11=16$$
$$1+1=9$$
$$4+4=8$$
$$10+10=20$$
$$6+4=10$$

MY MATH GOAL IS . . .

I wo todomr

Jobs

e

TEACHER NOTES:

Janeim will practice his doubles at school by using the number line, his fingers, bears, glass beads, and flash cards. He wants to use toys and flash cards to practice doubles at home.

FIGURE 11 Janeim's written goal at the end of the year was to practice his doubles.

WHAT HAPPENS IN MY CLASSROOM

LESSON ON SETTING GOALS: THE VERY QUIET CRICKET
VIDEO CLIP G

This clip shows *The Very Quiet Cricket* lesson in action in Dana's kindergarten classroom. *Before watching the clip, consider:*

- How would you introduce the concept of goal setting to your students?

As you watch the clip, consider:

- What is the role of children's literature in this lesson?
- How is the task of writing goals clarified before students begin working?
- What is the role of the teacher in this lesson? The students?
- How is the previous assessment data important to guide students as they set goals?
- Why does Dana ask students questions about their goals and record responses? Think specifically about her questions regarding what each student will do at school to meet his or her goal, what each student will do at home, and who will work with each student in each context.

In my school, some professional development days are dedicated to jigsawing (a cooperative learning technique) and discussing chapters in *7 Habits of Highly Effective People* (Covey 2004). I was sent—with two other teachers from my school—to visit a "Leader in Me School" in Florida, English Estates Elementary, which was implementing a school wide focus on the seven habits. At this time, my entire school is using the seven habits with the students. I embrace the seven habits because they reinforce and strengthen work I have been doing with my students and their families. The second of these habits is: *Begin with the end in mind.* In my classroom, I help students translate *Begin with the end in mind* into setting attainable academic goals. Putting an early childhood twist onto this means the goals must be attainable in a short amount of time. In order for young children not to give up, we must make sure they can see the results of their hard work and dedication. I involve parents with the process. I want students and parents from my classroom to believe that the education process is a partnership that involves the teacher, the student, and the parents. Parents help students reach their goals, and celebrate when their child does reach his or her goal. I have told families about Covey's book, and I believe our school will be offering a class for parents on the seven habits soon. We were just awarded a 21st Century Community Learning Center grant which allows us to offer after-school classes to students. One of the classes offered is about the seven habits and a parent class is on the table for discussion.

SECTION III

Lessons Integrating the Seven Formative Assessment Practices

FORMATIVE ASSESSMENT THROUGH GAMES

Games have numerous benefits. They are a fun way to provide practice and reinforcement of important mathematical content knowledge and processing skills, they are beneficial in reinforcing the procedures and expectations in a classroom setting, and they help develop a sense of community, which is crucial to learning in all content areas.

TEACHING TIP:
PLAYING GAMES

The first few times students play a new game, they are focused on learning the procedures of the game. Play the games many times with your students to emphasize the mathematical concepts embedded in each lesson.

The games included in this resource are games students want to play over and over again! They were created through the process of formative assessment in my classroom. If I notice during a lesson that my students are not mastering the content, I try to determine why this is happening. In some cases, language needs to be developed. Sometimes my students need more time and experience. Sometimes the "text" is asking students to use multistep procedures and students, in turn, become overwhelmed and miss the mathematical ideas. Through these games, I maintain the mathematical focus while simultaneously creating a bridge to student understanding, which ultimately leads to student success.

Keeping in mind the mathematical goals behind each game helps students make the connection between learning and a playful experience. Incorporating the use of teacher and student checklists (included in each lesson) is one way to help the teacher and students realize the mathematical learning taking place while still having fun together!

The Games

Many of these games are played in a whole-group setting (see page 3 for more on the reasoning behind whole-group lessons). Each game can be done as a lesson or during a transition time. The following is a brief overview of each game included in this section:

G-1 *The Attribute Game* (page 38): During this game, students work in a whole-group setting to guess, sort, and classify attributes that a group of their peers has in common.

G-2 *Guess My Pattern* (page 44): This game explores and studies the concept of pattern by having students, in a whole-group setting, physically become the pattern.

G-3 *Building Quantities on a Ten-Frame* (page 51) ⊙ The use of a life-size ten-frame in this game has students actively involved as both counters (counting) and "counters" (students stand on the ten-frame to represent the given quantity).

G-4 *+1, –1 on a Ten-Frame* (page 59) ⊙ This game introduces students to the symbols +1 and –1 and the actions that the symbols represent. Like G-3 *Building Quantities on a Ten-Frame,* it uses a life-size ten-frame.

G-5 *Practicing Combinations* (page 67): This game encourages the practice and reinforcement of combinations, starting with combinations of five.

G-6 *Shake and Spill Combinations* (page 73): This game revisits combinations of number while emphasizing the importance of recording in mathematics.

G-1 THE ATTRIBUTE GAME

Related Lessons

Consider as a follow-up lesson L-4 *The Button Box*.

Overview

During this game, students work in a whole-group setting to guess, sort, and classify attributes that a collection of their peers has in common. To do so, students must focus on details that are similar within a group or set. Students learn to make observations and strengthen their vocabulary to describe their ideas. They use logic and a process of elimination to verbalize appropriate descriptions of a given set. As each round continues, the possibilities of the shared attribute narrow, and students refine their guesses. Throughout, students build on an important mathematical skill: using what they know to figure out what they do not know. This game can be played as early as the first day of school and can be revisited throughout the year.

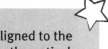

Aligned to the mathematical practices in the **Common Core State Standards**

Common Core State Standards

Measurement and Data: Standard K.MD

Describe and compare measurable attributes.

Classify objects and count the number of objects in each category, and sort the categories by count.

Goals for Student Understanding

These goals are aligned to the mathematical practices in the Common Core State Standards. Students will

- Make sense of problems and persevere in solving them.

- Construct viable arguments and critique the reasoning of others.

- Model with mathematics.

- Attend to precision.

- Look for and make use of structure.

Setting Whole group	*The Attribute Game* Student Checklist, 1 copy per student
Time Approximately ten to fifteen minutes	**Key Vocabulary** attributes do not have have same
Materials *The Attribute Game* Teacher Checklist	

TEACHING DIRECTIONS

1. Ask students to sit flat on their bottoms, legs crisscrossed, in a circle area.

2. Look for an attribute that several students have in common. Examples might be a blue shirt, a shirt with a collar, a shirt with buttons, shoes with Velcro, and so forth. When I introduce this game to my students, I choose an attribute that may be easier for students to discover; I do this because I first want to establish and focus on the procedures of the game. I often start with a specific shirt color. As students become comfortable and more confident in articulating their thinking, I increase the level of difficulty by focusing on more minute details.

3. Without stating the attribute, ask those students who share the attribute to stand and come to the front of the circle area. Make sure they can be seen easily by the seated students.

4. Encourage all students to look closely at those who are standing. Ask students the following key questions. Students try to discover and describe the common attribute. Students take turns guessing until someone names the attribute.

Key Questions

- What do these friends have in common?

- What are they wearing that is the same?

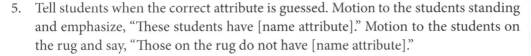

---

5. Tell students when the correct attribute is guessed. Motion to the students standing and emphasize, "These students have [name attribute]." Motion to the students on the rug and say, "Those on the rug do not have [name attribute]."

6. Repeat Steps 1 through 5 with a different attribute.

Extensions

Students Choosing the Attribute

Have a student be responsible for choosing an attribute and ask students who share that attribute to come up and stand (to do this, the student will have to practice sorting and categorizing). When I do this extension, I ask the student choosing the attribute to whisper the attribute into my ear first. This way, I can provide support as necessary.

Incorporating Number

This game provides a meaningful context for incorporating number sense in a variety of ways. Here are a few ideas:

- Have students represent numbers. Count the children standing and form a statement such as, "Five children have striped shirts." Then write the number 5 for everyone to see and connect the written numeral to the number word.

- Compare, for example, groups of children with stripes and without stripes. Which "set" is more? Less? How many children do not have a shirt with stripes?

- Establish that the number of students present is equal to the number of students with striped shirts plus the number of students without striped shirts. Describe this with a number

TEACHING TIP: THE WORD ATTRIBUTE

When introducing new vocabulary, say the new word and ask students to repeat the word. Then define the word and use it in a sentence. Next ask students to use the word in a sentence. Whenever possible, use visuals of physical examples to make the experience multisensory. In the case of the word *attribute*, I define it as "a characteristic that someone or something has." I tell my students, "My attribute is black pants because I am wearing black pants today. Can you use the word attribute in a sentence as you describe an attribute you have?" For more on teaching key vocabulary, see Section I, page 6.

TEACHING TIP: SEATING STUDENTS

I ask students to sit flat on their bottoms, legs crisscrossed, because sometimes I even look at their shoes to determine the attribute. I tell this to students as well as remind them that when they sit flat, everyone has a better chance of seeing what those who are standing are wearing.

sentence or an equation. For example, "There are eighteen students in our class. Five students have striped shirts; thirteen do not have striped shirts. We can also say, eighteen equals five plus thirteen."

FORMATIVE ASSESSMENT IN ACTION: QUESTIONS

Use these questions to help guide your observations of students as they engage in the lesson. Your focused observations support the instructional decisions you'll make for individual students and your class.

- Does the student participate? At what level?

- Does the student predict the attribute?

- Does the student refine his or her prediction with additional information?

- Does the student share his or her ideas during think-pair-share?

- Can the student categorize into sets (have the shared attribute and does not have the shared attribute)?

- Is the student able to select an attribute and sort for other students to predict their chosen attribute?

- Can the student connect numbers to *The Attribute Game?* Orally? With numerals? With an equation?

STUDENTS WHO STRUGGLE

Helping Students Who Do Not Share Their Predictions

TEACHING TIP: STUDENT PARTICIPATION

Students are even more engaged when they become part of the game—in this case, when they share the common attribute. Adapt games with this idea in mind.

After observing students play this game, you may notice a child who is not volunteering to make predictions. There could be a variety of reasons for this behavior. He or she may not be willing to take a risk in front of his or her peers yet. He or she may be an English learner who needs more oral language experiences to feel comfortable sharing ideas in front of others. This student may benefit from sorting and classifying activities with the teacher or another adult modeling the process and enriching the experience with vocabulary. Objects to sort might include nuts (in their shells), buttons, keys, or seashells.

Ensure that such students are part of the game by choosing an attribute each student has and building the set around that child's attribute. The goal is to draw even the most reluctant students into the game at some level of participation. With repeated experiences and consistent emphasis on the fact that we all learn from each other, even the most reluctant students find their place and their voice within the classroom.

WHAT HAPPENS IN MY CLASSROOM

TEACHING TIP: FREQUENCY

The Attribute Game can be played often (even as a transition) and should continue to include several rounds each time it is played.

While playing this game I help students see the role they play in their educational success. My expectations are that everyone participates by choosing an attribute to be guessed, verbalizing their ideas, or coming up to the front of the class as part of the group that shares an attribute. I also give students immediate feedback after they state their description of a set. If the student's description is incorrect, I will give justification such as, "It can't be short sleeves, because Taylor has short sleeves and I didn't ask her to stand up." Another student may guess that the shared attribute is "pants with pockets on the leg." Someone else may guess that it is "the color blue that my friends have in common." After a few incorrect guesses, I emphasize the importance of the information we learned from each other: "We learn from all of the guesses. Now what information do we have about what these friends have in common?" Students may express that they know the attribute is not short sleeves, pants with pockets on the leg, or the color blue.

I facilitate the whole-group discussion through the questions I ask. I want students to use what they know to figure out what they do not know. I want the next guess to be made by using the information we have about the set of students standing. To help students practice this process I ask them, "Talk to someone next to you. Using what we know now and looking closely at your classmates standing, what attribute do they share?" Using a think-pair-share is helpful to students, because it gives them a chance to refine their ideas, clarify their choice of words, and practice sharing their ideas. This experience allows everyone to feel more prepared and comfortable in sharing their thinking in front of the whole class. During think-pair-share, I listen to the conversations children are having. After students have a chance to communicate their ideas to each other, I begin eliciting responses from the class.

Using a think-pair-share is helpful to students, because it gives them a chance to refine their ideas, clarify their choice of words, and practice sharing their ideas.

When a student predicts correctly, I model classifying the set by saying, "You guessed my attribute! This set of friends has shoes with Velcro," and motion to the children standing. Then I point out, "This set of friends does not have shoes with Velcro" and motion to the seated students. Verbalizing the attribute that the children standing share, and distinguishing this from the set of seated children, helps students develop vocabulary to describe and classify sets. I might also ask students to echo (I make a statement, students repeat the statement) the classifications of the standing students and the seated students.

FORMATIVE ASSESSMENT IN ACTION: TEACHER AND STUDENT CHECKLISTS

The Attribute Game Teacher Checklist

Checklists are invaluable in helping to focus your observations as well as to document student behaviors, responses, and reactions to lessons. Each column in the checklist specifies what to observe while students are engaged in the mathematical activity. Having the checklist ready on a clipboard, and easily accessible, helps to ensure necessary documentation and recording takes place. For more on using teacher checklists as a successful formative assessment practice, see page 15.

The Attribute Game Student Checklist

This checklist helps students monitor their own learning, set math goals, and ultimately share academic progress with their parents. Each child should have his or her own student checklist and should keep it in his or her student notebook. For more on using student checklists (including video clips) as a successful formative assessment practice, see page 20.

Teacher Checklist: The Attribute Game

Student Names and Date	Participates Only When Asked	Predicts Attribute/ Refines Prediction	Discusses During Think-Pair-Share	Categorizes Attributes Have, Have Not	Sorts to Choose Attribute to be Guessed	Notes

STUDENT CHECKLIST

THE ATTRIBUTE GAME

NAME _____

I participate.	I make predictions.	I share my ideas with others.	I classify the sets.	I choose an attribute for others to guess.

DATE _____

DATE _____

DATE _____

DATE _____

 From *How to Assess While You Teach Math: Formative Assessment Practices and Lessons, Grades K–2: A Multimedia Professional Learning Resource* by Dana Islas. © 2011 Scholastic Inc. Permission granted to photocopy for nonprofit use in a classroom or similar place dedicated to face-to-face educational instruction.

G-2 GUESS MY PATTERN

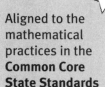

Related Lessons

Consider as a follow-up lesson L-5 *Hide and Snake*.

Overview

This game explores and studies the concept of pattern by having students become the pattern. In beginning experiences, the teacher creates the pattern and asks students to come up to the front of the class one by one. Students think about and figure out the pattern, then verbalize it. As students' understanding of pattern grows, the patterns that students are able to recognize, describe, and extend become more sophisticated. Ultimately students create the pattern. This game can be played throughout a unit of study involving pattern.

Aligned to the mathematical practices in the **Common Core State Standards**

Common Core State Standards

Although pattern is not explicitly referenced in the Common Core State Standards, such experiences are pivotal in creating a foundation for number, repeated addition, and multiplication.

Goals for Student Understanding

These goals are aligned to the mathematical practices in the Common Core State Standards. Students will

- Construct viable arguments and critique the reasoning of others.
- Make sense of problems and persevere in solving them.
- Construct viable arguments and critique the reasoning of others.
- Model with mathematics.
- Attend to precision.
- Look for and make use of structure.

Setting
Whole group.

Time
Approximately fifteen minutes.

Materials
Guess My Pattern Teacher Checklist
Guess My Pattern Student Checklist,
    1 copy per student

Key Vocabulary
repeating pattern
unit

TEACHING DIRECTIONS

1. Gather students in the whole-group area in your classroom. Explain to students that you will be creating a pattern with them.

2. Choose one student at a time to come toward the front of the whole-group area. As students come forward, create a pattern with them. The pattern can be created based on their clothing (specific color, stripes, shorts, and so on) or from a particular body position. For example, you may ask the first student to come up and stand. Then ask the next student to come up and sit, ask the third student to come up and stand, and so forth. Students will form a line, creating an AB pattern of stand, sit, stand, sit.

3. Have students who are seated look closely at the students in front. Ask them, "Can you guess the pattern created?"

4. When the pattern is verbalized, ask students, "What would come next in the pattern?"

5. When a student replies, "Stand!" ask this student to come up and *stand* to join the pattern.

6. Ask, "Now what would come next in this pattern?" When a student answers, "Sit," ask this student to come up and *sit* to join the pattern.

7. Continue adding to the pattern. Include as many students as you'd like and ask the following key questions:

Key Questions

- Is this a pattern? Why? Why not?
- What would come next in the pattern?
- Now what would come next in the pattern?.

---

8. Afterward, "read" the entire pattern to the class by tapping each corresponding student, "Stand, sit, stand, sit . . . ."

9. Play several rounds of this game in each session.

Extensions

Students Create the Pattern

Give students the opportunity to create the pattern. Have one student think of a pattern and whisper the pattern in your ear so you can provide support as necessary. Then have the student ask other students to come to the front of the class. The student will build his or her pattern. After the pattern is created, the student will ask the rest of the class to figure out the pattern. The student who created the pattern may also ask for his or her pattern to be extended. Students can be asked to describe the pattern or come up to show the unit or part of the pattern that repeats.

Students Create a Pattern Dance

For this extension, give each student a set of *Pattern Dance* pieces (see Reproducible G: *Pattern Dance*, at the end of the book), a glue stick, and paper. Explain to students that they need to create their own pattern using the pieces. The pieces represent movements that can be modeled by the teacher and students. Ask that students choose a minimum of two movements (for example, the girl jumping and the boy kicking) to create a pattern. After students have completed their patterns, gather the class and ask the students to form a circle in the whole-group area. Post their papers one at a time. Together, act out (dance!) the pattern movements in each of the posted papers. After each dance, ask students, "Is this a pattern? Why? Why not?"

FIGURE 12 In the *Guess My Pattern* game, Isabella's pattern used pieces from Reproducible G: *Pattern Dance*.

FORMATIVE ASSESSMENT IN ACTION: QUESTIONS

Use the following questions to help guide your observations of students as they are engaged in the lesson. These focused observations in turn support the instructional decisions you'll make for individual students and your class.

- Can the student determine whether this is a pattern?
- Can the student describe what makes this a pattern?
- Does the student know what comes next in this pattern?
- Can the student create a pattern for others to guess?
- Does the student recognize the unit or part that keeps repeating?

WHAT HAPPENS IN MY CLASSROOM

I use this game to introduce repeating patterns to students. Some students quickly grasp the idea that a pattern repeats; others need more experiences with this concept. The range of possibilities for student participation, as well as types of patterns that can be made, lend themselves nicely to differentiation within this game.

After I model the procedure of reading the pattern (gently tapping each student as I say what makes the pattern), I have found it helpful to have a student be the person to read the pattern. I ask the others to read along or choral the pattern.

The *Pattern Dance* extension is one way of recording and expressing a pattern. This lesson is of one of my students' favorites because they create and record a pattern for the whole class to get up and do together. One afternoon in my class, students made more *Pattern Dances* during their choice time. As they finished, they placed their dance on the rocker. We then "danced" together after cleaning up. The principal came in during cleanup and stayed for our dances. He was noticeably impressed with my students' explanations of why a dance was a pattern, why another dance was not a pattern, and how it could be changed. The students were having fun, bubbling over to express their explanations. What a great time for a visitor!

STUDENTS WHO STRUGGLE

Helping Students Recognize a Pattern

Consider the following two activities for students who struggle with recognizing a pattern.

Cubes in a Tube

To do this activity, adapted from *Supporting English Language Learners in Math Class, Grades K-2* (Bresser, Melanese, and Sphar 2008), you'll need interlocking cubes, an empty paper towel tube, and a bag. Using different-color cubes, create several patterns (for example, AB, AABB, ABBA, ABC). Also, create two sticks of randomly arranged cubes that are not a pattern. Place all the cube sticks you created in a bag so students cannot see them. Gather students together. Out of sight, take one pattern stick from the bag and place it in the paper towel tube. Reveal the stick, one cube at a time, pointing to the cube and stating the color until a color repeats. For example, "Maroon, yellow, maroon. What do you think will come next?" Elicit ideas from students, then confirm their predictions by revealing the next cube. Continue until all the cubes in the pattern stick are predicted, revealed, and confirmed. Ask students, "Is this a pattern?" When students agree that it is a pattern ask, "Why?"

Repeat this using one of the sticks that you put together randomly. Ask students if they are able to predict what will come next. Emphasize that there is no way to predict, because it is not a repeating pattern.

Small-Group Version of Guess My Pattern

Children struggling to recognize a pattern may benefit from small-group work. Consider playing a small-group version of *Guess My Pattern* with math manipulatives such as cubes, two-color counters, or pattern blocks. Begin the game by creating a pattern. Sit with the small group and ask them to look closely at the pattern and read it with you. "Blue, yellow, blue, yellow, blue, yellow. What color do you think will come next?" Ask the student who replies correctly (in this case, "blue") to add a blue cube/counter/block to the pattern. Continue this process until each student in the group has had a turn adding to the pattern. Then point to each cube and have students read the pattern with you. When you feel it's appropriate, turn the pattern creating over to the students; have each child take a turn building a pattern for the others to extend.

FORMATIVE ASSESSMENT IN ACTION: TEACHER AND STUDENT CHECKLISTS

Guess My Pattern Teacher Checklist

Checklists are invaluable in helping to focus your observations as well as to document student behaviors, responses, and reactions to lessons. Each column in the checklist specifies what to observe while students are engaged in the mathematical activity. Having the checklist ready on a clipboard, and easily accessible, helps to ensure necessary documentation and recording takes place. For more on using teacher checklists as a successful formative assessment practice, see page 15.

Guess My Pattern Student Checklist

This checklist helps students monitor their own learning, set math goals, and ultimately share academic progress with their parents. Each child should have his or her own student checklist and should keep it in his or her student notebook. For more on using student checklists (including video clips) as a successful formative assessment practice, see page 20.

Teacher Checklist: Guess My Pattern

Student Names and Date	Recognizes a Pattern	Can State Why It Is a Pattern	Extends Pattern/Predicts Next Stage	Can Show the Unit That Repeats	Creates a Pattern	Notes

Guess My Pattern

STUDENT CHECKLIST

NAME _____

	I recognize a pattern.	I know why it is a pattern.	I can extend a pattern.	I know where the unit repeats.	I can create my own pattern.

DATE _____

DATE _____

DATE _____

DATE _____

G-3 BUILDING QUANTITIES ON A TEN-FRAME

Related Lessons

Consider teaching first L-2 *Five Little Speckled Frogs.*
Consider as follow-up lessons G-4 *+1, −1 On a
Ten-Frame* and P-1 *How Many Frogs?*

Overview

This game provides a wonderful context for reinforcing vocabulary and introducing the ten-frame as a valuable mathematical tool to students. Students connect number names to written numerals and build sets to represent the given quantity on a ten-frame. The use of a life-size ten-frame has students actively involved as both counters (counting) and "counters" (students stand on the ten-frame to represent the given quantity). The discussions and immediate feedback that takes place during the game highlight student understandings and discoveries in a meaningful context.

Common Core State Standards

Counting and Cardinality: Standard K.CC

Know number names and the count sequence.

Count to tell the number of objects.

Compare numbers.

Aligned to the mathematical practices in the **Common Core State Standards**

Goals for Student Understanding

These goals are aligned to the mathematical practices in the Common Core State Standards. Students will

- Make sense of problems and persevere in solving them.

- Construct viable arguments and critique reasoning of others.

- Model with mathematics.

- Use appropriate tools strategically.

- Attend to precision.

- Look for and make use of structure.

- Look for and express regularity in repeated reasoning.

Setting

Whole group

Time

Approximately twenty minutes

Materials

Reproducible H: Number Cards 1–10,
    1 set of cards

1 life-size ten-frame (see Teaching Tip)

Building Quantities on a Ten-Frame
    Teacher Checklist

Building Quantities on a Ten-Frame Student
    Checklist, 1 copy per student

Key Vocabulary

add

count all

count back

count on

numeral

quantity

remove

represent

ten-frame

TEACHING DIRECTIONS

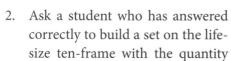

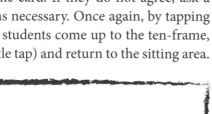

1. Gather students in the whole-group area in your classroom (where you've created your life-size ten-frame). Draw a card from a deck of number cards 1 through 10 (see Reproducible H). Ask students what numeral is on the card.

2. Ask a student who has answered correctly to build a set on the life-size ten-frame with the quantity represented by the numeral on the card. To do this, the student needs to tap seated students. As each student is tapped, he or she comes forward and stands in a square on the ten-frame. The designated student continues to tap seated students until the quantity on the ten-frame matches the numeral on the card.

3. Ask the students if they agree that the number of students on the ten-frame matches the quantity represented by the numeral on the card. If they do not agree, ask a volunteer to explain and change the quantity as necessary. Once again, by tapping students gently, the student should have more students come up to the ten-frame, or have students leave the ten-frame (via a gentle tap) and return to the sitting area.

> **Key Question**
>
> • Does the number of students on the ten-frame match the quantity on the card? Why not?

4. Draw another card and repeat Steps 1 through 3 several times.

TEACHING TIP: LIFE-SIZE TEN-FRAME

Create a life-size ten-frame in your whole-group area by using masking tape or colored tape (blue painter's tape works well). Make your ten-frame large enough for one student to be able to stand in each square. Choose a location toward the front or the side of your whole-group area that will allow all students to be able to see.

REPRODUCIBLE H

Extension

Using Ten-Frames and Counters

After the procedures of this game are familiar, have students play as a whole group using their own ten-frames and counters. When using their own ten-frames, students should sit in a circle. (When students are seated in a circle, it is easier to observe the strategies students are using as each set is built.) As the teacher, draw a card and have students create the quantity on their ten-frames. As in the original directions, have students share their thinking and strategies. After students are familiar with using their own ten-frames in this game, have them play individually or with a partner.

> **TEACHING TIP: ADDITIONAL RESOURCES**
>
> For more games using ten-frames, see *It Makes Sense! Using Ten-Frames to Build Number Sense* by Melissa Conklin.

FORMATIVE ASSESSMENT IN ACTION: QUESTIONS

Use the following questions to help guide your observations of students as they are engaged in the lesson. These focused observations in turn support the instructional decisions you'll make for individual students and your class.

- Is the student willing to share his or her thinking? In which settings (individual, partner, small group, or whole group) do you see the student as most comfortable in verbalizing his or her mathematical thinking?

- Does the student understand that there are 10 squares on the ten-frame? Five on the top row and five on the bottom row?

- Does the student use this information when building on the ten-frame?

- How does the student build on the ten-frame? Left to right? Top row to bottom row? In groups of two, one on the top row and one on the bottom row?

- Does the student represent the given quantity accurately?

- Does the student represent a new quantity efficiently by adding on or removing from the previous quantity?

STUDENTS WHO STRUGGLE

Helping Students Who Are Unwilling to Share Their Thinking

Some students may not be ready to share their thinking. If I ask a student to share and the student is not willing or able to explain his or her thinking to the class, I might try to verbalize the student's thinking. For example, if Andrea is hesitant to share her thinking, I might say, "I noticed Andrea adding on when she built seven on the ten-frame. Why do you think she added on instead of wiping the ten-frame clean, and then building a new set with seven?" By noticing Andrea's strategy and validating that other people are using her way of thinking, I hope to draw Andrea further into the game. With repeated experiences using a ten-frame in this type of setting, Andrea will eventually be encouraged to verbalize her own ideas. Make clear to the class your expectation that everyone is an important part of learning time; we learn from each other!

Helping Students with Representing a Quantity Accurately

Counting is complex. Children need many experiences counting a variety of objects to develop successful counting strategies. Such counting strategies include being organized, touching each object as it is counted, using one-to-one correspondence, conserving, and double-checking. A combination of student-directed experiences and planned, purposeful experiences helps students become aware of what good "counters" do. Quick images, Rekenreks (bead boards), ten-frames, counting each other, and counting snacks are all opportunities that will help students become better counters and become better at representing quantities accurately.

WHAT HAPPENS IN MY CLASSROOM

BUILDING QUANTITIES ON A TEN-FRAME

VIDEO CLIP H

In this clip, Dana describes the community aspects, benefits, and goals of this game, as well as the types of responses she is interested in seeing from her students. The clip then shows students playing the game on the floor-size ten-frame in Dana's kindergarten classroom. *As you watch the clip, consider:*

- How does Dana use the floor-size ten-frame to build an understanding of number concepts with her students?
- What strategies do students use to build and/or adjust a quantity?
- What questions does Dana ask to help build an understanding of composing and decomposing numbers?

After you watch the clip, consider:

- How does playing this game in a whole-group setting impact student learning?
- What benefits does a floor-size ten-frame provide students?

Often when students are introduced to ten-frames they count all the counters for each new quantity. Each time, they wipe their ten-frame clean and build the next quantity by counting all. I carefully watch for students who are acknowledging that there are five squares on the top row of their ten-frame and five squares on the bottom row. When I notice this I ask, "Why would that be helpful to remember when playing this game?" Students reach a mathematical milestone after they internalize that there are five on the top row and five on the bottom row, and thus they do not need to count each object within a square every time to know how many are on the ten-frame.

Intentional discourse between students and teacher during this game can encourage children to count on or count back to build a new quantity. When I notice a student adding on or removing from the original set to build a new quantity, I validate and highlight this strategy by talking about it and writing it down. I might say, "I noticed you added on to the students already on the ten-frame. Why did you add on?" For example, if there are seven students standing on the ten-frame, one of my students may respond, "I know I have five and I can add six then seven to make seven" (as the student points to the two students added on). I have also heard, "There are five and two more makes seven." Strategies I have observed my students using include counting all, counting on, and counting back. I make a list of the strategies *used by the students* to acknowledge and emphasize the use of strategies as well as to encourage vocabulary development.

As students explain their thinking and justify their strategies, they solidify their thinking. Other students are given a different perspective on a way to approach the situation. Students who have not tried the strategy can be asked to try it when the next quantity is built. I check in with a student trying a new strategy by asking key questions:

Key Questions

- Does the strategy of counting on work? Why?
- Do we need to clear the ten-frame every time we build a new set? Why not?

After several more quantities are built, I ask my class questions like the following:

Key Questions

- Is it quicker to count on or to count back from the counters on the ten-frame?
- Is it quicker to clear the ten-frame and then build the new set?

The discussions that take place enhance the learning for all students. Through these discussions, immediate feedback is given and new strategies are tried. Students are empowered to use new vocabulary to communicate their understandings to others. All students benefit from this by speaking, listening, considering new possibilities, and understanding that their voice is important. Allowing time for communication and additional practice gives students the information and reinforcement they need to strengthen their mathematical understandings. In turn, as the teacher I gain insights to the concepts students understand and those that students need additional support with and practice to master (formative assessment in action!).

FORMATIVE ASSESSMENT IN ACTION: TEACHER AND STUDENT CHECKLISTS

Building Quantities on a Ten-Frame Teacher Checklist

Checklists are invaluable in helping to focus your observations as well as to document student behaviors, responses, and reactions to lessons. Each column in the checklist specifies what to observe while students are engaged in the mathematical activity. Having the checklist ready on a clipboard, and easily accessible, helps to ensure necessary documentation and recording takes place. For more on using teacher checklists as a successful formative assessment practice, see page 15.

Building Quantities on a Ten-Frame Student Checklist

This checklist helps students monitor their own learning, set math goals, and ultimately share academic progress with their parents. Each child should have his or her own student checklist and should keep it in his or her student notebook. For more on using student checklists (including video clips) as a successful formative assessment practice, see page 20.

TEACHER CHECKLIST: BUILDING QUANTITIES ON A TEN-FRAME

Student Names and Date	Recognizes Numbers	Builds Set	Builds Top Left–Right/ Bottom Left–Right	Removes All, Then Builds New Set	Builds from Counters Already on Ten-Frame	Notes

 From *How to Assess While You Teach Math: Formative Assessment Practices and Lessons, Grades K–2: A Multimedia Professional Learning Resource* by Dana Islas.
© 2011 Scholastic Inc. Permission granted to photocopy for nonprofit use in a classroom or similar place dedicated to face-to-face educational instruction.

BUILDING QUANTITIES ON A TEN-FRAME

STUDENT CHECKLIST

NAME _____

	I recognize numbers.	I build sets.	I build top, left to right, then bottom, left to right.	I build from the counters already on the ten-frame.

DATE _____

DATE _____

DATE _____

DATE _____

From *How to Assess While You Teach Math: Formative Assessment Practices and Lessons, Grades K–2: A Multimedia Professional Learning Resource* by Dana Islas.

G-4 +1, -1 ON A TEN-FRAME

Related Lessons

Consider teaching first G-3 *Building Quantities on the Ten-Frame*.

Overview

This game introduces students to the symbols +1 and –1 and the actions that the symbols represent. The use of a life-size ten-frame has students actively involved as both counters (counting) and "counters" (students stand on the ten-frame to represent the given quantity). Playing this game in a whole-group setting helps students transfer an understanding of +1, –1 to partner or individual games and paper/pencil settings (see, for example, Figure 19 on page 123 and Figure 24 on page 134). The discussions and immediate feedback that take place during the game highlight student understandings and discoveries in a meaningful context.

Common Core State Standards

Counting and Cardinality: Standard K.CC

> *Know number names and sequence.*

> *Count to tell the number of objects.*

> *Compare numbers.*

Operations and Algebraic Thinking: Standard K.OA

> *Understand addition as putting together and adding to, and understand subtraction as taking apart and taking from.*

Operations and Algebraic Thinking: Standard 1.OA

> *Work with addition and subtraction equations.*

Aligned to the mathematical practices in the **Common Core State Standards**

Goals for Student Understanding

These goals are aligned to the mathematical practices in the Common Core State Standards. Students will

- Make sense of problems and persevere in solving them.

- Reason abstractly and quantitatively.

- Construct viable arguments and critique the reasoning of others.

- Model with mathematics.

- Use appropriate tools strategically.
- Attend to precision.
- Look for and make use of structure.
- Look for and express regularity in repeated reasoning.

Setting

Whole group

Time

Approximately fifteen minutes

Materials

number cards 1 through 10, 1 set
Reproducible I: +1, –1 cards, cut apart to
form one deck of 10
1 life-size ten-frame
+1, –1 on a Ten-Frame Teacher Checklist
+1, –1 on a Ten-Frame Student Checklist,
    1 copy per student

Key Vocabulary

add
less
minus one
more
numeral
quantity
plus one
represent
subtract
ten-frame

TEACHING DIRECTIONS

TEACHING TIP: LIFE-SIZE TEN-FRAME

Create a life-size ten-frame in your whole-group area by using masking tape or colored tape (blue painter's tape works well). Make your ten-frame large enough for one student to be able to stand in each square. Choose a location toward the front or the side of your whole-group area that will allow all students to be able to see.

1. Gather students in the whole-group area in your classroom (where you've created your life-size ten-frame). Draw a card from a deck of number cards 1 through 10. Ask students what numeral is on the card.

2. Ask a student who has answered correctly to build a set on the life-size ten-frame with the quantity represented by the numeral on the card. To do this, the student taps seated students. As each student is tapped, he or she comes forward and stands in a square on the ten-frame. The designated student continues to tap seated students until the quantity on the ten-frame matches the numeral on the card.

3. After the quantity is built, draw a card from a deck of +1, –1 cards. Ask students about the symbol on the card, "Does the symbol on the card mean that we need one more or one less?" After the meaning of the symbol is established, ask a student either to add one more student to the ten-frame (if a +1 card is drawn) or remove one student (if a –1 card is drawn). Remind students to tap students gently either to add them to or remove them from the ten-frame.

4. Ask students, "What is the new quantity on the ten-frame?" Verify with students how many students are on the ten-frame. This discussion time is a valuable opportunity to double-check the final quantity, use new vocabulary, connect abstract

symbols to concrete experiences, clarify confusion, and discuss the effects of addition and subtraction on a whole number.

5. Restate the equation made from drawing the number card; the +1, −1 card, and the total. For example, if the number card is 5 and a +1 card is drawn, creating a total of six, state, "Five plus one equals six."

6. Draw another card and repeat Steps 1 through 5 several times. Keep asking the key questions.

Key Questions

-   Does the symbol on the card mean that we need one more or one less?
-   What is the new quantity on the ten-frame?

Extensions

Connecting Abstract Symbols

Some children may become fluent with *+1, −1 on a Ten-Frame* very quickly. An appropriate extension for children with this understanding may be to connect them with a written representation of the equation. During each round of the game, write the equation where everyone in the class can see it. These written representations connect abstract symbols to the concrete experiences of the game.

Combinations of Ten

With repeated experiences, students learn to recognize each row of the ten-frame as a group of five. Some students become very aware of 10 as they focus on the spaces filled on the ten-frame, whereas others see the negative or unfilled spaces. Capitalize on students' discoveries of number relationships within 10 by writing number sentences that capture students' thinking. For example, write *10 = 5 + 5* to represent that the ten-frame has five on the top row and five on the bottom row. For a ten-frame in which seven squares have counters and three squares are empty, write *7 + 3 = 10*.

FORMATIVE ASSESSMENT IN ACTION: QUESTIONS

Use these questions to help guide your observations of students as they are engaged in the lesson. Your focused observations in turn support the instructional decisions you'll make for individual students and your class.

-   Does the student connect the numeral to the number word?
-   Can the student create a set to represent the numeral?

TEACHING TIP: WRITING EQUATIONS

Using variation when writing equations helps students become flexible in their understanding that an equation shows a balanced relationship between the numbers. Make an effort to say "is the same as" in place of "equals" when reading the equation.

- Does the student demonstrate an understanding of more and less, and represent this understanding on the ten-frame?
- What strategies does the student use to find the new quantity? Count all? Count on? Count back?

STUDENTS WHO STRUGGLE

Helping Students Connect the Numeral and the Number Word

Students who are not yet making a connection between the numeral and the number word need more experiences in understanding the purpose for knowing this connection. Playing popular card games such as *Go Fish* and *Concentration* using number cards can support the needs of these students. I've found these types of practice to be meaningful and motivational in helping children to acquire this necessary skill.

Helping Students Understand More and Less

Some students may still be confused about the meaning of more and less, even after playing this game. Playing card games such as *War* (also known as *More*) using number cards and counters can support the needs of these students. For counters, consider using interlocking cubes. These cubes allow for a physical model of the quantities on the cards to be made. Students can then directly compare their cube stick with the quantity on the card.

When I ask students to sign in on a graph to collect data, this provides another opportunity for supporting students' understanding of more and less. Look at the data on the sign-in graph in a whole-group setting. This is a real life context to examine the idea and meaning of more, less, and the same. Incorporate interlocking cubes into this experience for the purposes of having a physical model. A hundreds chart and a number line are other tools that can be used to look at the relationships between numbers and the concept of more and less.

WHAT HAPPENS IN MY CLASSROOM

+1, –1 ON A TEN-FRAME

VIDEO CLIP 1

In this clip, Dana describes how she introduces the game, the goals of the game, and what she looks for as students play the game. The clip then shows students playing the game on the floor-size ten-frame in Dana's classroom. *As you watch the clip, consider:*

- How does Dana use this game to build on student understandings of number concepts?

- How does + 1, – 1 on a floor-size ten-frame give students an experience of addition and subtraction?

After you watch the clip, consider:

- How would you use this opportunity to formatively assess your students?

Students often confuse the meaning of the symbols + and – when they are introduced. Students also grapple with an understanding of more and less, and the effect of more or less on whole numbers. An abstract introduction to symbols can complicate this confusion. In my classroom, this game helps eliminate confusion by providing a meaningful context that immediately immerses students in the exploration of number. The fact that students are central to the game (they are, physically, the counters on the ten-frame) usually increases their eagerness to participate. The whole-group setting allows me to ask questions of all my students as they are playing the game. I often reinforce prior ten-frame knowledge by asking students, "How many squares are on the top row? The bottom row? How many squares are on the ten-frame?" I constantly listen to students' responses and observe students' behavior to check for understanding. Students continually receive immediate feedback from their peers and from me. Students are usually quick to respond if they disagree and are willing to help their classmates understand why they disagree.

I give students ample time to practice and process the experience through purposeful dialogue. I always ask the student how he or she figured out the total amount. Sometimes a child says, "I just know." If this happens, I ask the student more questions and probe for information to gain insight into his or her thinking. Sometimes a child will count all, count on, or count back to find the total. All strategies are valid, because they are useful in finding the amount in the new set. As this game unfolds, students may double-check their response and use one-to-one correspondence. Both are skills that good counters use; I make sure I comment on and reinforce this. I highlight efficient strategies through thoughtful questions and encourage others to try the new strategies, especially as students learn the effects of addition and subtraction on whole numbers. It's important to make sure the strategies come from the children. It's my role as the teacher to emphasize and bring these strategies to the attention of the rest of the class. I encourage my students to borrow one another's strategies.

> *Sometimes a child says, "I just know." If this happens, I ask the student more questions and probe for information to gain insight into his or her thinking.*

Through meaningful, well-planned experiences and discussions during this game, students recognize that they play a role in their own learning as well as the learning of others. I've found that this game works especially well after other experiences using the ten-frame in a whole-group setting, with a partner, or individually at a table.

FORMATIVE ASSESSMENT IN ACTION: TEACHER AND STUDENT CHECKLISTS

+1, –1 on a Ten-Frame Teacher Checklist

Checklists are invaluable in helping to focus your observations as well as to document student behaviors, responses, and reactions to lessons. Each column in the checklist specifies what to observe while students are engaged in the mathematical activity. Having the checklist ready on a clipboard, and easily accessible, helps to ensure necessary documentation and recording takes place. For more on using teacher checklists as a successful formative assessment practice, see page 15.

+1, –1 on a Ten-Frame Student Checklist

This checklist helps students monitor their own learning, set math goals, and ultimately share academic progress with their parents. Each child should have his or her own student checklist and should keep it in his or her student notebook. For more on using student checklists (including video clips) as a successful formative assessment practice, see page 20.

TEACHER CHECKLIST: +1, –1 ON A TEN-FRAME

Student Names and Date	Connects Number Word to Numeral	Creates a Given Set	Demonstrates Understanding of + as More, – as Less	Represents +1, –1 on Ten-Frame	Counts All to Find Total	Counts on, Counts Back to Find Total	Notes

NAME _____

+1, −1 ON A TEN-FRAME

I understand +1, −1.	I represent +1, −1.	I count all to find the total.	I count on or count back to find the total.

DATE _____

DATE _____

DATE _____

DATE _____

G-5 PRACTICING COMBINATIONS

Related Lessons

Consider teaching first G-6 *Shake and Spill Combinations*. Consider as a follow-up lesson P-2 *Combinations of Ants and Grapes*.

Overview

This game encourages the practice and reinforcement of combinations, starting with combinations of five. The teacher shows students five tiles, then hides some of them. Students figure out how many tiles are hidden based on the number of tiles that remain. The game reinforces the strategies of counting all and counting on. Discussions during the game support connections between concrete experiences, oral communication, and symbols. As the game is repeated, it provides a natural and meaningful context to introduce equations.

Common Core State Standards

Counting and Cardinality: Standard K.CC

Count to tell the number of objects.

Operations and Algebraic Thinking: Standard K.OA

Understand addition as putting together and adding to, and understand subtraction as taking apart and taking from.

Operations and Algebraic Thinking: Standard 1.OA

Work with addition and subtraction equations.

Aligned to the mathematical practices in the **Common Core State Standards**

Goals for Student Understanding

These goals are aligned to the mathematical practices in the Common Core State Standards. Students will

- Make sense of problems and persevere in solving them.

- Reason abstractly and quantitatively.

- Construct viable arguments and critique the reasoning of others.

- Model with mathematics.

- Attend to precision.

- Look for and make use of structure.

- Look for and express regularity in repeated reasoning.

Setting

Whole group

Time

Approximately fifteen to twenty minutes

Materials

5 color tiles
Practicing Combinations Teacher Checklist

Practicing Combinations Student Checklist, 1 copy per student

Key Vocabulary

combinations
counting all
counting on
equals

TEACHING DIRECTIONS

TEACHING TIP: MANIPULATIVES

Although tiles are referenced in this lesson, any manipulative small enough to conceal in your hand can be used to play this game.

TEACHING TIP: DIFFERENTIATING YOUR INSTRUCTION

You can easily adjust the number of tiles you choose to hide to meet the varying needs of your students.

1. Gather students in the whole-group area in your classroom. Ask them to sit in a large circle.

2. Place five tiles in a line on the floor. Count the tiles out loud with students.

3. Explain to students that you are going to hide some of the tiles. Their job is to look at the remaining tiles and predict how many tiles are hidden.

4. Ask students to close and cover their eyes. Remind them, no peeking! After students have their eyes closed and covered, hide two tiles.

5. Then tell your students, "Open your eyes and count the tiles on the floor." Ask them, "How many tiles are hidden?" Elicit responses from them.

6. When a student responds, "Three," ask, "How do you know that three are hidden?" Depending on the student's response, verify or ask the student to verify with the rest of the class. Model the strategy of counting all or counting on. Say, "Let's count together by *counting all*—one, two, three, four, five," and "Let's *count on*—three, four, five."

7. Reveal the hidden tiles to students. Verbalize the equation: "Five tiles equals (is the same as) two tiles plus three tiles."

8. Repeat Steps 1 through 7 several more times, hiding different quantities of tiles each time until all the combinations are revealed. Continue asking the following key questions:

Key Questions

- How many tiles are hidden?
- How do you know that ___ are hidden?

Extensions

Adding More Tiles

When students are familiar with the procedures of the game and have had substantial experience with combinations of five, consider adding other tiles to the mix (I usually go up one number—from using five tiles to six, and so on up to ten).

Connecting the Concrete Experience to Written Representation

When students become very fluent with the combinations of a given number, introduce them to equations that represent the concrete experiences they have had. I explain to students that they have been describing their thinking by using words and sentences; they can also describe their thinking by using number sentences or equations. I model writing equations to correspond with a concrete physical model. For the round described in the teaching directions, write *5 = 2 + 3* after eliciting responses from students and revealing the hidden titles. If a student describes the reason they know is by counting all, capture the student's words in symbols by writing *1, 2, 3, 4, 5*. Note the strategy by writing *counting all*. If a student describes the strategy of counting on, write *3, 4, 5* and *counting on*.

FORMATIVE ASSESSMENT IN ACTION: QUESTIONS

Use the following questions to help guide your observations of students as they are engaged in the lesson. Your focused observations in turn support the instructional decisions you'll make for individual students and your class.

- Does the student conserve the total number of counters?

- What strategy does the student use to determine the quantity hidden? Counting all? Counting on? Does the student know the combinations of the original quantity?

- Can the student describe orally the concrete experience using numbers?

- Can the student represent the concrete experience by writing a number sentence?

STUDENTS WHO STRUGGLE

Helping Students with Conservation

Usually I begin with the quantity of five with my kindergarten students. If a student is having difficulty with this quantity, I reduce the amount of tiles to meet his or her individual needs. After the student is comfortable with a smaller quantity, I increase the amount of tiles by one and work with the child until he or she gains an understanding of and confidence in the new quantity.

> **TEACHING TIP: LITERATURE CONNECTION**
>
> A great literature connection for combinations of seven is *Quack and Count* by Keith Baker.

> **TEACHING TIP: WRITING EQUATIONS**
>
> Using variation when writing equations helps students understand that an equation shows a balanced relationship between the numbers. Make an effort to say "is the same as" in place of "equals" when reading the equation.

Helping Students Make Connections to Written Number Sentences

Students need many concrete experiences before making connections to written number sentences. If a student is struggling with this component, continue to immerse the child in hands-on experiences in counting objects (see G-3 *Building Quantities on a Ten-Frame* and G-6 *Shake and Spill Combinations*).

WHAT HAPPENS IN MY CLASSROOM

I keep a set of ten color tiles with my teaching materials at our whole-group circle area at all times. This enables me to use this game often during transitions. It is a quick, worthwhile game that needs very little setup. I adjust it to meet the changing needs of students. As we begin each round I emphasize, "Close your eyes, cover your eyes." I want students to use what they know to figure out what they do not know. I do not want them to peek! I make it clear that I value efforts made in trying to figure out what isn't known. I want students to see themselves as problem solvers. I reiterate the message of using what you know to figure out what you do not know through many experiences, including this game, over time.

See page 13 for insights on using a hiding assessment in individual assessments.

While my students are enjoying this game as a whole class, I am gaining valuable information, including which students know their combinations, which strategies students are using to figure out how many tiles are hidden, and which students still need substantial help to develop an understanding of number relationships. My students help extend each other's thinking through their explanations (as I facilitate the questioning) more than I could push their thinking by modeling these strategies myself!

FORMATIVE ASSESSMENT IN ACTION: TEACHER AND STUDENT CHECKLISTS

Practicing Combinations Teacher Checklist

Checklists are invaluable in helping to focus your observations as well as to document student behaviors, responses, and reactions to lessons. Each column in the checklist specifies what to observe while students are engaged in the mathematical activity. Having the checklist ready on a clipboard, and easily accessible, helps to ensure necessary documentation and recording takes place. For more on using teacher checklists as a successful formative assessment practice, see page 15.

Practicing Combinations Student Checklist

This checklist helps students monitor their own learning, set math goals, and ultimately share academic progress with their parents. Each child should have his or her own student checklist and should keep it in his or her student notebook. For more on using student checklists (including video clips) as a successful formative assessment practice, see page 20.

TEACHER CHECKLIST: PRACTICING COMBINATIONS

Student Names and Date	Conserves Total Quantity	Counts All	Adds On	Knows Combinations	Writes Combinations	Notes

STUDENT CHECKLIST

NAME _____

COMBINATIONS of _____

I count all.	I count on.	I know my combinations.	I write number sentences to represent combinations.

DATE _____

DATE _____

DATE _____

DATE _____

G-6 SHAKE AND SPILL COMBINATIONS

Related Lessons

Consider teaching first G-5 *Practicing Combinations*. Consider as a follow-up lesson P-2 *Combinations of Ants and Grapes*.

Overview

This game, adapted from the lesson *Shake and Spill* in *About Teaching Mathematics: A K–8 Resource, Third Edition* (Burns 2007), provides an opportunity to practice and reinforce the combinations of five, with the option to adjust the quantity as students gain understanding. The game also emphasizes the importance of recording in mathematics. The game can be played in a variety of settings (whole group, small group, partners, or even individually). To play, the teacher or students shake and then spill a container containing five two-color counters. Students represent each of their spills by recording the color of the corresponding number of counters on their recording sheets. As the game is repeated, it provides a natural and meaningful context to introduce equations.

Common Core State Standards

Counting and Cardinality: Standard K.CC

Count to tell the number of objects.

Operations and Algebraic Thinking: Standard 1.OA

Add and subtract within 20.

Work with addition and subtraction equations.

Measurement and Data: Standard 1.MD

Represent and interpret data.

Measurement and Data: Standard 2.MD

Represent and interpret data.

Aligned to the mathematical practices in the **Common Core State Standards**

Goals for Student Understanding

These goals are aligned to the mathematical practices in the Common Core State Standards. Students will

- Make sense of problems and persevere in solving them.

- Reason abstractly and quantitatively.

- Construct viable arguments and critique the reasoning of others.

- Model with mathematics.
- Use appropriate tools strategically.
- Attend to precision.
- Look for and make use of structure.
- Look for and express regularity in repeated reasoning.

Setting

Whole group, small group, partners, or individually

Time

Approximately fifteen minutes

Materials

5 two-color counters (red and yellow), 1 set per group of players

small bowl for the counters, 1 per group of players

yellow and red crayons for each group of players

Reproducible F: *Shake and Spill* Recording Sheet, 1 copy per student

Shake and Spill Combinations Teacher Checklist

Shake and Spill Combinations Student Checklist, 1 copy per student

Key Vocabulary

combinations

equation

number sentence

TEACHING TIP: MODELING SHAKE AND SPILL

To avoid potential chaos with shaking and spilling the counters, model shaking and spilling the counters on the table in front of you several times. Afterward, strategically ask several students to model the appropriate manner to shake and spill the counters.

TEACHING DIRECTIONS

1. Explain to students that they will be playing a game called *Shake and Spill*. This game will give them another opportunity to explore combinations of five.

2. Describe and model shaking and spilling. Place five two-color counters in a container. Shake the container and spill all the counters. Spill the counters such that they stay in front of you (rather than across the table or onto the floor).

3. Explain to students that you will not be saving the two-color counters after each spill, so they will need to record the counter colors of each spill on a recording sheet (see Reproducible F: *Shake and Spill* Recording Sheet). Model coloring one section of the recording sheet to represent the spill. For example, if the counters landed with four red and one yellow, color four circles red and one circle yellow on the recording sheet. Recording the equations with red and yellow markers helps everyone see how the two-color counters landed and distinguishes between the combinations.

4. Decide whether you will have students play the game as a whole group, small group, in partners, or individually. Emphasize that students are to shake and spill four times, recording after each spill.

5. Distribute containers with two-color counters, copies of the recording sheet, and crayons. Have students play until they have filled their recording sheets.

6. When all students have finished, have students share results in a whole-group setting if appropriate. As students share, connect the concrete experience of each shake and spill to symbols by writing the list of equations for everyone to see. For example, $5 = 0 + 5, 5 = 1 + 4, 5 = 2 + 3, 5 = 3 + 2, 5 = 4 + 1, 5 = 5 + 0$. Consider color coding the numbers in red and yellow: $5 = 0$ (red) $+ 5$ (yellow) and $5 = 5$ (red) $+ 0$ (yellow).

Extensions

Changing the Number of Counters

The number of two-color counters can be changed as the needs of students change. For example, if students know the combinations of five, proceed to combinations of six (use six two-color counters).

Using the List of Equations as Data to Examine

After all equations have been recorded for the class to see, examine these data as a whole group. Questions to think about when examining class data include the following:

> ### *Key Questions*
>
> - Which combinations occurred most often?
> - Which combinations occurred least often?
> - Why do you think this is happening?

Applying What Students Know to Different Situations

Games like this one and G-5 *Practicing Combinations* reinforce combinations of a given number. Consider giving students an opportunity to apply their growing understanding of combinations through problem-solving experiences (see, for example, lesson P-2 *Combinations of Ants and Grapes*). After a particular problem is solved, have students share their strategies. This discussion will help students make connections between the experiences they have had playing the games and applying what they have learned to solve a problem.

FORMATIVE ASSESSMENT IN ACTION: QUESTIONS

Use the following questions to help guide your observations of students as they are engaged in the lesson. Your focused observations in turn support the instructional decisions you'll make for individual students and your class.

- Is the student able to record outcomes of the spill accurately? How does the student record color? Numerals? Equations?

- With which combinations is the student fluent? Which combinations does the student need more time to explore?

TEACHING TIP: MATH JOURNALS

To accommodate the various times that students may finish their recording sheets, consider asking students who have finished to write about the experience in their math journals.

TEACHING TIP: CONNECTING SPILLS TO SYMBOLS

A student's first experience should not include the connection of the symbols to represent each spill. This connection is made after students have had many concrete experiences exploring and discussing the combinations. This game provides a meaningful context to introduce the symbols when students revisit the game.

- Does the student apply what he or she knows about combinations to problem-solving situations?

STUDENTS WHO STRUGGLE

Helping Students See the Value of Recording Their Work

Young children often want to save whatever it is they have worked on—whether it be block buildings, Lego structures, or pattern-block designs. Any time students want to save something they have made, encourage them to draw a picture, write down a description in words, and/or use paper pattern blocks and glue sticks (for pattern-block designs) to save their work. Emphasize that it is not always possible to save the real structure or design, therefore they need to represent it as closely as possible for future enjoyment and conversation.

These experiences and conversations provide real-life opportunities for students to understand the importance of recording. A record creates a permanent artifact that can be saved and shared with others (including students' parents). Abundant experiences with recording help students see the value and the usefulness of it, as well as enhance students' abilities to represent and communicate mathematically.

WHAT HAPPENS IN MY CLASSROOM

I find it beneficial to offer students repeated experiences with this lesson in the form of an independent center. Students understand the procedures; playing the game in an independent center gives them the opportunity to practice and reinforce the math concepts. I am able to observe and record on the spot when students are working in small groups, with partners, and individually. I often ask students to draw and write about their experience with math centers in their math journal. I feel this helps make the important connection between writing and math while providing a purposeful writing prompt.

Shake and Spill lends itself nicely to differentiation. The number of counters can be adjusted as well as the level of recording. Students who are ready to write numerals or equations to represent the results of their spills can do so, whereas students who need to place each counter onto the recording sheet, then color accordingly, can also have that opportunity.

FORMATIVE ASSESSMENT IN ACTION: TEACHER AND STUDENT CHECKLISTS

Shake and Spill Teacher Checklist

Checklists are invaluable in helping to focus your observations as well as to document student behaviors, responses, and reactions to lessons. Each column in the checklist specifies what to observe while students are engaged in the mathematical activity. Having the checklist ready on a clipboard, and easily accessible, helps to ensure necessary documentation and recording takes place. For more on using teacher checklists as a successful formative assessment practice, see page 15.

Shake and Spill Student Checklist

This checklist helps students monitor their own learning, set math goals, and ultimately share academic progress with their parents. Each child should have his or her own student checklist and should keep it in his or her student notebook. For more on using student checklists (including video clips) as a successful formative assessment practice, see page 20.

TEACHER CHECKLIST: SHAKE AND SPILL

Student Names and Date	Accurately Records Spill	Writes Numbers to Record Spill	Writes Equations to Record Spill	Notes

SHAKE AND SPILL

STUDENT CHECKLIST

NAME _____

I record my spill.	I write numbers to record my spill.	I write number sentences to record my spill.

DATE _____

DATE _____

DATE _____

DATE _____

FORMATIVE ASSESSMENT THROUGH MATH AND LITERATURE

As early childhood teachers, we are drawn to children's literature. Great children's books help us build themes and make connections across the curriculum. I especially celebrate the connections when I discover how to make a favorite children's book become a favorite math lesson. In this section I share six of these favorite lessons.

Some books initially seem to be simple counting books. I've learned that it's often these books that can be invaluable springboards for purposeful lessons in creating mathematical foundations. These foundational books and ideas can be built on and revisited so they evolve with students as students' mathematical skills and understandings grow.

Reading Books: The Importance of Repeated Experiences

On a bookcase in my classroom I keep picture books that go nicely with the themes and standards about which my students are learning. I select books to read during whole-group settings in the morning (such as Morning Circle), before lunch, and in the afternoon (Closing Circle). I want students to hear the book several times before I use it for a context of a lesson. This allows students to focus on a new aspect of the story. During read-alouds I ask students to make predictions about the cover of the book, the characters, and the setting. I model turning pages carefully. I talk about the parts of a book, such as the front and back cover, the end papers, title page, and spine. I tell students who the author and illustrator are, and sometimes ask, "What does the author do? What does the illustrator do?" When students have had a chance to hear a book several times, with many of these routines having taken place, students pay more focused attention to the mathematical task when it is introduced. Before reading a book for mathematical purposes, I make a statement or ask students a question to guide their attention. For example, before reading *Lottie's New Beach Towel*, I tell students that the main character, Lottie, is a great problem solver, and then I ask students to listen to find out what Lottie does to be a problem solver.

Formative Assessment in These Lessons

The following lessons were created through a process of formative assessment in my classroom. If I notice during a lesson that my students are not mastering the content, I try to determine why this is happening. In some cases, language needs to be developed. Sometimes my students need more time and experience. Sometimes the additional language and experience can be within the context of literature. Through these lessons, I maintain a mathematical focus through lessons that the children choose to revisit. These additional experiences help students reinforce understandings and make connections to other mathematical lessons they encounter within a unit of study. This creates a bridge to student understanding, which ultimately leads to student success.

Keeping in mind the mathematical goals behind each lesson helps students make the connection between a great book and learning more about mathematics. Incorporating the use of teacher and student checklists, included in each lesson, is one way to help the teacher and students realize the mathematical learning that is taking place while still having fun together!

The Lessons

The following is a brief overview of each math- and literature-based lesson included in this section:

L-1 *Ten Black Dots*, page 82: The *Read It, Say It, Make It, Write It* format of the lesson prompts students to interact with quick images in a variety of ways to develop number concepts, including grouping quantities rather than counting by ones.

L-2 *Five Little Speckled Frogs*, page 89 In the delightful rhyming book *Five Little Speckled Frogs,* five frogs sitting on a log gulp bugs and jump into a pool one by one. The story serves as the lesson's springboard for helping students represent the characters and the actions taking place.

L-3 *Color Zoo*, page 97: How many animals can you create in the color zoo? This lesson creates a beautiful connection between mathematics, art, and literature, ultimately providing practice in exploring shapes.

L-4 *The Button Box*, page 104: The children's book *The Button Box* provides a delightfully imaginative context for this lesson. After hearing the story read, students work with a partner to sort and classify their set of ten buttons.

L-5 *Hide and Snake,* page 112: *Hide and Snake* by Keith Baker is a mosaic adventure that invites readers to trace a snake's movements as it slithers through yarn, hats, cats, and more. This bright, visually engaging book sets the context for students to create their own pattern-block snakes.

L-6 *Lottie's New Beach Towel,* page 119: The delightful adventures in *Lottie's New Beach Towel* inspire the problem solver in every student. Lottie is thoughtful, resourceful, and a very good problem solver! Students then take their turn at being problem solvers.

L–1 TEN BLACK DOTS

Related Lessons

Consider as a follow-up lesson P-4 *My Name in Color Tiles!*

Overview

Donald Crews's *Ten Black Dots* provides a visually rich exploration in answering the question, "What can you do with ten black dots?" (One dot can make a sun, two dots can make the eyes of a fox, and more.) This lesson uses Crews's book as the premise for an introduction to quick images. The *Read It, Say It, Make It, Write It* format of the lesson prompts students to interact with quick images in a variety of ways to develop number concepts, including grouping quantities rather than counting by ones.

Common Core State Standards

Aligned to the mathematical practices in the **Common Core State Standards**

Counting and Cardinality: Standard K.CC

Count to tell the number of objects.

Operations and Algebraic Thinking: Standard K.OA

Understand addition as putting together and adding to, and understand subtraction as taking apart and taking from.

Operations and Algebraic Thinking: Standard 1.OA

Add and subtract within 20.

Work with addition and subtraction equations.

Operations and Algebraic Thinking: Standard 2.OA

Add and subtract within 20.

Goals for Student Understanding

These goals are aligned to the mathematical practices in the Common Core State Standards. Students will

- Make sense of problems and persevere in solving them. Reason abstractly and quantitatively.

- Construct viable arguments and critique the reasoning of others.

- Model with mathematics.

- Use appropriate tools strategically.

- Attend to precision.

- Look for and make use of structure.

Setting

Whole group and small group

Time

Approximately twenty minutes

Materials

Ten Black Dots by Donald Crews
two-color counters, 10 per student
individual small whiteboards and
whiteboard markers, 1 per student
(or paper and pencils)

Reproducible J: Quick Image Cards
Ten Block Dots Teacher Checklist
Ten Black Dots Student Checklist,
    1 copy per student

Key Vocabulary

clump
compose
decompose
equation
represent

TEACHING DIRECTIONS

Part 1: Read It

1. Gather students in the whole-group area in your classroom. Introduce (or reread) the familiar book *Ten Black Dots*. Explain to students that you will be sharing quick images with black dots.

Part 2: Say It

2. Show students one of the quick-image cards (see Reproducible J). Give students about three seconds to study the dot image on the card (count to three slowly in your head). Then hide the card. Repeat this process with the same card, then ask students, "What did you see?" Encourage students to clump the dots rather than count by ones. Emphasize the importance of looking for a variety of groupings that will make up the same quantity.

3. Repeat Step 2 using three or four different quick-image cards.

Part 3: Make It

4. When students are familiar with *Say It* quick images, tell them they are going to *Make It*. This time they will make what they see when you show the quick image. In this case, have students sit in small groups at tables. Place two-color counters in the center of each table (ten per student).

5. As you did in Step 2, show students a quick-image card and slowly, silently count to three. Hide the card. Ask students, "What did you see?" Using counters, students should make what they saw. When the students are done, show the card again, this time quickly. Ask students to make any necessary adjustments to their counters.

> **TEACHING TIP: ENJOYING LITERATURE**
>
> Familiarize students with the story before introducing the math lesson. The first time a book is read, it should be listened to and enjoyed. Students can make connections to other concepts after they have had a chance to absorb the story.

REPRODUCIBLE J

6. Now tell students, "Describe what you saw." This is the time to make a connection to their ideas with symbols. Write number sentences describing the quantity represented in their arrangements. For example, students may say, "I saw two and two and two and two." In turn, write *8 = 2 + 2 + 2 + 2*. Another child may say, "I saw four and four." Write *8 = 4 + 4.*

Key Questions

- What did you see?
- Describe what you saw.

Part 4: Write It

7. *Write It* follows *Say It* and *Make It* with quick images. This time, when you show students a card, ask them to describe in writing the way they saw the arrangements. Some students will draw what they saw in the quick image, some students will write numbers, and others will write an equation.

Extensions

Using Color Tile Quick Images

Quick images with color tile arrangements offer the same concept with a different manipulative. Color tile quick images are a nice bridge to the lesson P-4 *My Name in Color Tiles!* Make color tile quick images by gluing paper color tile arrangements onto 4 by 6-inch unlined index cards. I use color tile quick images many times before introducing the lesson *My Name in Color Tiles!* to students.

Other Literature Connections: Five Creatures by Emily Jenkins

In this book, a young girl describes her five family members (three humans and two cats) in many different ways. Her descriptions are perfect segues to exploring numbers.

After reading *Five Creatures*, use quick-image cards to represent the combinations illustrated in the one- and two-page spreads in the book. This can be especially helpful for students needing additional support. After reading *Five Creatures* several times in a whole-group setting, have students make a quick image that represents the characters in the story. Select several pages from the story to read again (one-page or two-page spreads at a time). Ask students to create a quick image based on the information they hear.

FORMATIVE ASSESSMENT IN ACTION: QUESTIONS

Use the following questions to help guide your observations of students as they are engaged in the lesson. Your focused observations in turn support the instructional decisions you'll make for individual students and your class.

- How does the student decompose the quantity? Does the student try to find several different ways to decompose the quantity?

- Is the student able to recreate the arrangement?

- What does the student write to show how he or she decomposed the arrangement? Pictures? Numbers? Equations? Words?

STUDENTS WHO STRUGGLE

Helping Students Who Count by Ones

Some students may describe the arrangement by counting with ones. I acknowledge that this is a possibility, but I also encourage them to look for clumps of dots that are easy to see and keep track of. I also talk to students about being efficient. I share two examples with an image by asking students to compare whether it is quicker and easier to keep track of

$$1 + 1 + 1 + 1 + 1 + 1 \text{ or } 2 + 2 + 2$$

$$1 + 1 + 1 + 1 + 1 + 1 \text{ or } 3 + 3$$

$$1 + 1 + 1 + 1 + 1 + 1 \text{ or } 4 + 2$$

Part of being a good mathematician is doing what makes sense, but also being efficient. With more time and experiences hearing other students describe the way they see arrangements, students counting by ones make a shift to looking for friendly groups of dots.

WHAT HAPPENS IN MY CLASSROOM

As students gain an understanding of my expectations during quick images, they become excited to share the way they saw an arrangement. Frequently, students want to share more than one way of seeing an arrangement.

I use quick images with dots when I introduce this idea to my students. Eventually I use color tiles to make arrangements. This leads to P-4 *My Name in Color Tiles!*, which is an absolute favorite in my classroom. Students love recording their name, and they take great pride in their ability to understand and record a mathematical connection to each letter.

> **TEACHING TIP: QUICK IMAGES**
>
> For more on using quick images, including video clips of their use in a kindergarten classroom, see Chapter 3 of *Number Talks: Helping Children Build Mental Math and Computation Strategies, Grades K-5* by Sherry Parrish (2010). In her book, the author refers to quick images as *dot cards*.

FORMATIVE ASSESSMENT IN ACTION: TEACHER AND STUDENT CHECKLISTS

Ten Black Dots Teacher Checklist

Checklists are invaluable in helping to focus your observations as well as to document student behaviors, responses, and reactions to lessons. Each column in the checklist specifies what to observe while students are engaged in the mathematical activity. Having the checklist ready on a clipboard, and easily accessible, helps to ensure necessary documentation and recording takes place. For more on using teacher checklists as a successful formative assessment practice, see page 15.

Ten Black Dots Student Checklist

This checklist helps students monitor their own learning, set math goals, and ultimately share academic progress with their parents. Each child should have his or her own student checklist and should keep it in his or her student notebook. For more on using student checklists (including video clips) as a successful formative assessment practice, see page 20.

TEACHER CHECKLIST: TEN BLACK DOTS

Student Names and Date	Decomposes Arrangements	Finds More Than One Way to Decompose	Recreates Arrangements	Describes Arrangement in Writing	Notes

 From *How to Assess While You Teach Math: Formative Assessment Practices and Lessons, Grades K–2: A Multimedia Professional Learning Resource* by Dana Islas. © 2011 Scholastic Inc. Permission granted to photocopy for nonprofit use in a classroom or similar place dedicated to face-to-face educational instruction.

STUDENT CHECKLIST

NAME _____

TEN BLACK DOTS

I decompose arrangements.	I recreate arrangements.	I describe arrangements.

DATE _____

DATE _____

DATE _____

DATE _____

L-2 FIVE LITTLE SPECKLED FROGS

Related Lessons

Consider as a follow-up lesson P-1 *How Many Frogs?*

Overview

In the delightful rhyming book *Five Little Speckled Frogs*, five frogs sitting on a log gulp bugs and jump into a pool one by one. The story serves as the lesson's springboard for helping students represent the characters and the actions taking place. Students first listen to the story while the teacher reads it aloud, then they act it out during a second reading. After this introductory experience, the teacher reads the story again, and this time students use cubes to represent the actions of the characters. Finally, after students are familiar with using manipulatives (cubes) to represent the story's actions, they connect the physical models with equations. By bringing *Five Little Speckled Frogs* into a math lesson, we capitalize on young children's willingness to act out their favorite rhymes. We also give them the opportunity to use objects as props in a dramatic-play setting. The use of literature as a tool makes representing with manipulatives seem very natural. Key questions like "How many frogs are on the log now?" help students maintain their representation and follow along with the story.

Common Core State Standards

Counting and Cardinality: Standard K.CC

Know number names and the count sequence.

Count to tell the number of objects.

Operations and Algebraic Thinking: Standard K.OA

Understand addition as putting together and adding to, and understand subtraction as taking apart and taking from.

Operations and Algebraic Thinking: Standard 1.OA

Add and subtraction within 20.

Work with addition and subtraction equations.

> Aligned to the mathematical practices in the **Common Core State Standards**

Goals for Student Understanding

These goals are aligned to the mathematical practices in the Common Core State Standards. Students will

- Make sense of problems and persevere in solving them.

- Reason abstractly and quantitatively.

- Model with mathematics.
- Use appropriate tools strategically.
- Attend to precision.
- Look for and make use of structure.

Setting

Whole group

Time

Approximately twenty minutes

Materials

Five Little Speckled Frogs by Nikki Smith
cubes, 5 per student
1 basket or container for holding and
    passing out the cubes
Reproducible S: *Five Little Speckled Frogs*
    Picture Cards (for the extension)

Five Little Speckled Frogs Teacher
Checklist
Five Little Speckled Frogs Student
    Checklist, 1 copy per student

Key Vocabulary

combinations
equation
number sentence
represent

TEACHING DIRECTIONS

Part 1: Reading the Book: Acting Out the Story

TEACHING TIP: GIVING EVERYONE A TURN

Act out the story throughout the week to allow all students to have a turn to be a frog. Keep up the list of students' names who have had a turn to act as a frog; this is a simple way to track who has had a turn. Students rarely tire of acting out their favorite rhymes; plus, the repeated experience gives students practice with the combinations of five.

1. Gather students in the whole-group area of your classroom. Prior to using this story as a launch for a math lesson, read the book *Five Little Speckled Frogs* to students to build their familiarity with it. In preparation for the lesson, tell students you will reread the story and this time, they will act it out. Ask students, "Who are the characters in this book? How many frogs are in the story?"

2. Write the word *frog* on the board five times in a list format. Ask students, "Who would like to be a frog?" Select five students to play frogs. Write each of the five students' names next to the word *frog*.

3. Ask the five students selected to come toward the front of the circle area and pretend that they are frogs sitting on a log.

4. Tell the students in the audience that you will be the narrator, but you will need them to help you tell the story.

5. Begin the story. "Five little speckled frogs, sitting on a hollow log . . . ." When you get to the part that reads, "One jumped into the pool . . . ," motion for one of the "frogs" to jump into the "pool." The student should pretend to frog-hop into the pool.

6. Ask students the following key questions. These questions help students maintain their representation and follow along with the story.

Key Questions

- How many frogs are on the log now?
- How many frogs are in the pool now?

7. Continue your role as narrator, reading the rhyme and asking key questions while the audience assists and the frogs on the log jump into the pool.

Part 2: Reading the Book: Representing with Cubes

8. Place five cubes per student in a basket or container that can be easily passed around. Ask students to sit in a large circle. Tell them that this time you have cubes for them to use in acting out the story. Students will typically be excited for another variation of this favorite rhyme.

9. Ask students the following key questions. After students respond, ask them to pass the basket around, each taking five cubes from it and placing the cubes in front of him or her on the floor.

Key Questions

- How many frogs are in the story?
- How many cubes will you need to act out this story?

10. Tell students that you will be the narrator again and they will need to help you tell the story. This time, however, as you tell the story, their cubes will be the frogs.

11. Ask students, "Where were the frogs in the beginning of the story?" When students have determined that the frogs were on a log, ask students to line up their cubes on their imaginary logs.

12. After students have their cubes (frogs) lined up in front of them, ask them, "What would happen if all of the frogs jumped into the middle of our circle area? Would we be able to keep track of all of the frogs very easily? Would there be one frog jumping in at a time?" (Make sure students realize that the pool is in front of their log, not in the middle of the circle area.)

13. Ask students, "What happens in the middle of this story?" After students respond that the frogs jump into the pool, ask, "How could you show this using your cubes?" Give students a minute to practice moving their frogs from their logs into their pools.

14. Begin reading the story. Students move one cube into the pool as you say, "One jumped into the pool where it was nice and cool." Each time a frog leaves the log to jump into the water, ask students the following key questions:

Key Questions

- How many frogs are on the log now?
- How many frogs are in the pool now?

Extensions

Retelling Five Little Speckled Frogs

Have students work alone or with a partner to retell the story of *Five Little Speckled Frogs* using picture cards (see Reproducible S: *Five Little Speckled Frogs* Picture Cards). Students aim to put the picture cards in order by counting and comparing the number of frogs on the log with the number of frogs in the pool. As an extension, students write equations to represent what is taking place on each card.

Reading the Book and Writing Number Sentences

After children are very familiar with the cubes as a form of representation, connect the physical model to equations. Tell students, "We can write sentences with words, but we can also write sentences with numbers. I heard you say there are four frogs on the log (write a *4* where everyone can see it) and there is one frog in the pool (write *+ 1* where everyone can see it). Ask, "How many frogs did we start with?" Record students' response of 5 by adding *= 5* after the *4 + 1*. Repeat this process, soliciting and recording a number sentence after each frog jumps into the pool:

$$4 + 1 = 5$$
$$3 + 2 = 5$$
$$2 + 3 = 5$$
$$1 + 4 = 5$$

Some children may be ready to record the actions of the story by writing the equations themselves.

Other Literature Connections

There are several other wonderful children's stories that can be used for teaching representation; they include the following:

Let's Go Visiting by Sue Williams

Mouse Count by Ellen Stoll Walsh

One Gorilla: A Counting Book by Atsuko Morozumi

Splash! by Ann Jonas

Ten Little Fish by Audrey Wood

The nursery rhyme *Five Little Monkeys* by Eileen Christelow

Quack and Count by Keith Baker

Five Creatures by Emily Jenkins

FORMATIVE ASSESSMENT IN ACTION: QUESTIONS

Use these questions to help guide your observations of students as they are engaged in the lesson. Your focused observations in turn support the instructional decisions you'll make for individual students and your class.

- Does the student volunteer to act out the story or does she or he prefer to be an audience member?
- Does the student use his or her cubes to represent accurately the action taking place in the story?
- Can the student record an equation that represents the actions taking place in the story?

STUDENTS WHO STRUGGLE

Helping Students with Representation Using Manipulatives

Students who are struggling with the idea of representing with manipulatives need more time and experiences. This can be done one-on-one, in a small group, or in a whole group using the same familiar stories. As the teacher, model using the cubes to represent the actions in the story and verbalize your actions. Ask students who are able to represent the story using a manipulative to describe what they are doing; this is also helpful for students who are struggling.

WHAT HAPPENS IN MY CLASSROOM

FIVE LITTLE SPECKLED FROGS
VIDEO CLIP J

In this clip, Dana describes how her students got hooked on this lesson—and how the mathematical twist encourages students to take the lesson further. The clip then shows the two parts of the lesson in action in Dana's classroom. *As you watch the clip, consider:*

- What is the role of children's literature in this lesson?
- What questions does Dana ask to help students' develop an understanding of number concepts?
- How do the expectations shift when students are asked to use cubes to represent the frogs?
- How does the use of cubes to represent the frogs give all students access to number concepts?

After you watch the clip, consider:

- How can this lesson evolve with the changing needs of the students?
- What is the importance of offering students repeated experiences?

I introduce the book *Five Little Speckled Frogs* to students during the first week of school. They quickly become familiar with the story and song. My students love acting it out! They will ask to act it out several times in a row to allow more students to have a chance to be a frog. When acting out any story, I explain the various roles students play; it's especially important for students in the audience to see that they have a role, too. As the audience, students should watch and listen to the performance, assist the narrator when appropriate, and applaud afterward. Students who are performing should play their parts, speak loudly (if they have speaking parts), have fun, and take a bow at the end. These expectations encourage students to take their roles as performers or audience members seriously. Defining roles also helps students make other connections. For example, students have a better appreciation for what an audience member should do while attending assemblies or field trips with a performance. The role of audience helps students understand what *audience* means when we are writing or communicating our thinking to others throughout different subject areas of the curriculum.

In my classroom, *Five Little Speckled Frogs* is a wonderful way to extend students' repertoire to representing with cubes. The situation is very familiar and we make a shift toward abstract representation. This shift leads to empowering students mathematically! The situation in the story/song changes and the students' representations change accordingly.

FORMATIVE ASSESSMENT IN ACTION: TEACHER AND STUDENT CHECKLISTS

Five Little Speckled Frogs Teacher Checklist

Checklists are invaluable in helping to focus your observations as well as to document student behaviors, responses, and reactions to lessons. Each column in the checklist specifies what to observe while students are engaged in the mathematical activity. Having the checklist ready on a clipboard, and easily accessible, helps to ensure necessary documentation and recording takes place. For more on using teacher checklists as a successful formative assessment practice, see page 15.

Five Little Speckled Frogs Student Checklist

This checklist helps students monitor their own learning, set math goals, and ultimately share academic progress with their parents. Each child should have his or her own student checklist and should keep it in his or her student notebook. For more on using student checklists (including video clips) as a successful formative assessment practice, see page 20.

TEACHER CHECKLIST: FIVE LITTLE SPECKLED FROGS

Student Name and Date	Uses Cubes to Represent Characters	Models Action of Characters with Cubes	Maintains Five Cubes Log to Pool	Records Number Sentences to Represent Story	Notes

STUDENT CHECKLIST

NAME _____

FIVE LITTLE SPECKLED FROGS

I represent the characters in the story using manipulatives.	I know my combinations of five.	I use number sentences to represent the characters in the story.

DATE _____

DATE _____

DATE _____

DATE _____

From *How to Assess While You Teach Math: Formative Assessment Practices and Lessons, Grades K–2: A Multimedia Professional Learning Resource* by Dana Islas.
© 2011 Scholastic Inc. Permission granted to photocopy for nonprofit use in a classroom or similar place dedicated to face-to-face educational instruction.

L-3 COLOR ZOO

Related Lessons

Consider teaching first G-1 *The Attribute Game.* Consider as a follow-up lesson P-5 *The Four-Triangle Problem.*

Overview

This lesson creates a beautiful connection between mathematics, art, and literature, ultimately providing practice in exploring shapes. In her book *Color Zoo,* Lois Ehlert uses bold colors and bright geometric shapes to create a variety of animals in the zoo. After hearing the story, students use precut paper geometric shapes to create their own animals in the style of Lois Ehlert. For a more challenging art project, the lesson suggests Lois Ehlert's bilingual book *Cuckoo.*

Common Core State Standards

Geometry: Standard K.G

Identify and describe shapes (squares, circles, triangles, rectangles, hexagons, cubes, cones, cylinders, and spheres).

Analyze, compare, create, and compose shapes.

Geometry: Standard 1.G

Reason with shapes and their attributes.

Geometry: Standard 2.G

Reason with shapes and their attributes.

Aligned to the mathematical practices in the **Common Core State Standards**

Goals for Student Understanding

These goals are aligned to the mathematical practices in the Common Core State Standards. Students will

- Make sense of problems and persevere in solving them.
- Model with mathematics.
- Use appropriate tools strategically.

Setting

Small group or whole group

Time

Approximately thirty minutes

Materials

Color Zoo by Lois Ehlert
precut, brightly colored paper geometric
    shapes
glue sticks
construction paper

Color Zoo Teacher Checklist
Color Zoo Student Checklist, 1 copy per
    student

Key Vocabulary

character
corners
curved lines
represent
shape names
sides
straight lines

TEACHING TIP: PREPARING THE SHAPES

Cutting the shapes for this lesson can be done by a parent or older student volunteers. Another possibility is to establish a cutting station where students cut shapes for practice and place the shapes in shape tubs (by shape) to be used at a later time. A quick means of cutting shapes is to staple several sheets of brightly colored copy paper together, then trace the attribute block shapes onto the paper. Choose a variety of shapes and sizes. Afterward, cut the shapes out and paperclip sets of shapes together (in other words, use a paperclip to group all the small triangles together, all the large rectangles together, and so forth).

TEACHING DIRECTIONS

Part 1: Reading the Book and Making Connections to Mathematics and Art

1. Gather students in the whole-group area in your classroom. Explain that you will be reading the familiar story *Color Zoo*. After the story is read, everyone will be representing a character (animal) from the story using shapes and the artistic style of Lois Ehlert, the author and illustrator. Ask students to listen to the story and think about which animal they might want to make, as well as which shapes they could use to represent the animal.

2. As you read the story, help students make connections to shapes in real-world objects. Ask students to look closely at a character on a page. Ask the following key questions:

Key Questions

- What shapes did Lois Ehlert use to make this character?
- Do the shapes stand alone or did she put shapes together to make different shapes?

Part 2: Creating Your Own Animal

3. After reading the story, ask students to do a think-pair-share, during which each student turns to the person next to him or her and shares the character he or she wants to make. Show students examples of precut shapes, glue sticks, and construction paper. Explain that these are the materials they will use to make their animal.

4. Model making a character, talking through the process as you make it.

5. Tell students that it is their turn to make an animal from the book. Have students work at tables. Make sure that there are plenty of paper shapes and glue sticks at each table.

6. As students finish their characters, have them either write in their math journal about this experience or make another character.

Part 3: Processing the Activity

7. When everyone has finished, gather students in a whole-group setting to process the activity. Choose several characters to discuss with the class. Draw attention to the types of shapes students used. Purposefully incorporate and model mathematical vocabulary. Ask students to describe the shapes. Some students may know the shape names; others may not. Look more closely at the shapes and ask students to describe what they see. Ask the following key questions:

Key Questions

- Is the shape made of straight lines or curved lines?
- Does the shape have corners? How many corners?
- What is a side? How many sides does this shape have?

Extensions

Using Cuckoo by Lois Ehlert

For a more challenging project, read the bilingual story *Cuckoo*. Instead of gluing shapes to paper to represent characters, have students connect the shapes using metal brads. When you reach Step 4, when modeling how to make the character, say, for example, "I am going to use this orange circle for my mole's head. I will connect it to this purple oval. The oval will be my mole's body. I am going to poke the brad through my paper circle and then through my oval to connect the pieces together." Note that some students may struggle with pushing the brads through the paper. There are also students who can push the brads through easily. Ask these students to assist others by explaining how they did it so easily. Consider using the end of a paperclip to poke a small hole through the paper. It's easier to push the brad through a hole that is already started in the paper. For examples of student work done for this extension, see the "What Happens in My Classroom" section.

Sorting Shapes

Give each student a set of 10 different shapes. Ask them to sort the shapes several different ways. Have students choose their favorite way to sort the shapes and then glue the shapes onto a piece of paper. Label the manner in which the shapes are sorted. Students may label with words, numbers, or equations.

FORMATIVE ASSESSMENT IN ACTION: QUESTIONS

Use these questions to help guide your observations of students as they are engaged in the lesson. Your focused observations in turn support the instructional decisions you'll make for individual students and your class.

- Does the student notice shapes in the environment?

- What vocabulary does the student use to describe the shapes? Curved lines, straight lines, corners, sides?

- Does the student know the names and characteristics of shapes? Does the student put shapes together to make other shapes?

STUDENTS WHO STRUGGLE

Beyond grappling with the brads, one of the wonderful things about this lesson is that there really is very little that students will struggle with. The fact that each student is creating his or her own animal meets each student at his or her level. It's a fabulous lesson for differentiating instruction. This lesson also gives students who are struggling in other areas a chance to shine!

WHAT HAPPENS IN MY CLASSROOM

I always make sure the shapes used in this lesson are precut and ready to go. Although many young children need to practice their fine motor skills and would benefit from cutting, I want the focus of this lesson to remain on mathematics—specifically, building vocabulary and exploring shapes.

Lessons such as this one remind me of the pride students take in their work. The engagement and energy level of students allow rich conversations to flow almost effortlessly. Although there is a framework for students to follow, they are entrusted with making a plan for their project, choosing shapes, and working toward completion. (See Figure 13.)

Students really can't go wrong as they place the shapes together to make a character. My role as the teacher is to point out which shapes students use to create the parts of the particular character being built, and to ask students why a particular shape was chosen. My questions and explorations help students make connections between shapes and real-world objects. For example, in addition to choosing specific shapes for her project, Gizelle was excited to use a yellow triangle for her bird's beak. Upon questioning her, she explained to me that the color yellow was the same color as Sydney's (our class pet) beak. I told her that I noticed she was careful to select all purple triangles for her bird's wings and tail; she clearly had a plan as to what her bird should look like. At another table, Isabella said, "Look! Two eyes!" I noticed what Isabella was seeing and shared with others that we had a view of Cynthia's bird that allowed us to see both of the circle-shaped eyes. Cynthia excitedly added on to my explanation; her bird could also open and close its mouth because she used two triangles. I pointed out that Cynthia used ovals to make her bird, and the neck and feet.

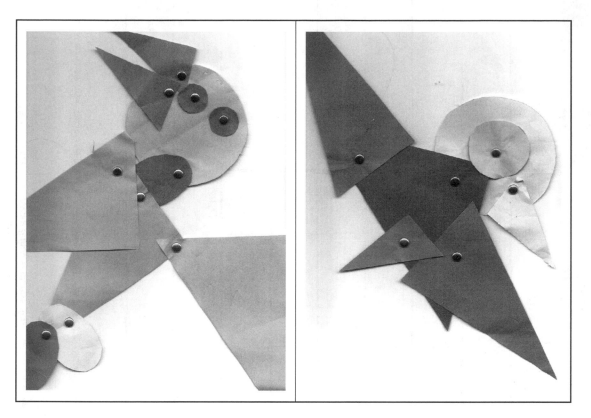

FIGURE 13 Students created shape animals for the extension using *Cuckoo* by Lois Ehlert.

FORMATIVE ASSESSMENT IN ACTION: TEACHER AND STUDENT CHECKLISTS

Color Zoo Teacher Checklist

Checklists are invaluable in helping to focus your observations as well as to document student behaviors, responses, and reactions to lessons. Each column in the checklist specifies what to observe while students are engaged in the mathematical activity. Having the checklist ready on a clipboard, and easily accessible, helps to ensure necessary documentation and recording takes place. For more on using teacher checklists as a successful formative assessment practice, see page 15.

Color Zoo Student Checklist

This checklist helps students monitor their own learning, set math goals, and ultimately share academic progress with their parents. Each child should have his or her own student checklist and should keep it in his or her student notebook. For more on using student checklists (including video clips) as a successful formative assessment practice, see page 20.

TEACHER CHECKLIST: Color Zoo

Student Names and Date	Recognizes Shapes in the Environment	Represents a Character by Putting Shapes Together	Vocabulary Used	Notes

STUDENT CHECKLIST

NAME

Color Zoo

I recognize shapes in my world.	I used shapes to represent a character in the style of Lois Ehlert.

DATE

DATE

DATE

DATE

L-4 THE BUTTON BOX

Related Lessons

Consider teaching first G-1 *The Attribute Game* and L-1 *Ten Black Dots*. Consider as a follow-up lesson P-4 *My Name in Color Tiles!*

Overview

The children's book *The Button Box* provides a delightfully imaginative context for this lesson. After hearing the story read, students work with a partner to sort and classify their set of ten buttons. They then record their two favorite ways to sort the set of ten buttons using pictures, words, numbers, and equations. In a whole-group setting, partners share their button sorts and the teacher records all the different equations students used to represent their thinking. Each equation demonstrates different ways a quantity of ten can be partitioned, helping students understand that, in this case, the quantity remains ten regardless of how it is partitioned.

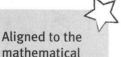

Aligned to the mathematical practices in the **Common Core State Standards**

Common Core State Standards

Measurement and Data: Standard K.MD

Classify objects and count the number of objects in each category.

Operations and Algebraic Thinking: Standard 1.OA

Represent and solve problems involving addition and subtraction.

Goals for Student Understanding

These goals are aligned to the mathematical practices in the Common Core State Standards. Students will

- Make sense of problems and persevere in solving them.

- Reason abstractly and quantitatively.

- Construct viable arguments and critique the reasoning of others.

- Model with mathematics.

- Use available tools strategically.

- Attend to precision.

- Look for and make use of structure.

- Look for and express regularity in repeated reasoning.

Setting

Whole group and partners

Time

Approximately forty-five minutes

Materials

The Button Box by Margarette Reid
10 buttons, 1 set for each pair of partners
Reproducible K: *The Button Box* Recording
   Sheet, 1 copy per student

The Button Box Teacher Checklist
The Button Box Student Checklist, 1 copy
   per student

Key Vocabulary

classify
equation
partition
sort

TEACHING DIRECTIONS

Part 1: Making Real-Life Connections

1. Explain to students that they will be thinking about sorting and classifying. One real-life example of sorting and classifying is food in the grocery store. Food is sorted so shoppers can find what they are looking for easily, and so foods can be properly stored (at the right temperature, for example). Frozen items are together in the freezer section, refrigerated items are in the refrigerated section, canned items are on the shelves, and so forth.

2. Ask students, "What is something in your house that is sorted? Why do you think it is organized this way?" Do a think-pair-share; give students a moment to think to themselves, then ask them to share their ideas with the person sitting next to them. Finally, ask students to share their ideas with the whole group.

3. Remind students of different sorting and classifying experiences they have had at school (an example may be the lesson G-1 *The Attribute Game* in this resource).

Part 2: Reading the Book *The Button Box*

4. Gather students in the whole-group circle area. Reread the familiar book *The Button Box*.

Part 3: Sorting Buttons

5. Explain to students that they will work with a partner to sort and classify buttons in many ways. Partners need to decide on their two favorite ways to sort the buttons, then record the sorts using pictures, words, numbers, and equations. All the buttons must be included in the sort. Give a copy of Reproducible K: *The Button Box* Recording Sheet to each student.

> **TEACHING TIP: DIFFERENTIATING YOUR INSTRUCTION**
>
> Adjust the number of buttons in the sets to meet your students' individual needs.

> **TEACHING TIP: PARTNERING STUDENTS**
>
> Thoughtful pairing of students can help all of them be successful. Three factors to always take into consideration are personality types, language ability, and mathematical strengths.

REPRODUCIBLE K

Part 4: Processing the Activity

6. After everyone has finished recording, gather students in the whole-group area.

7. Ask partners to take turns standing up and sharing the ways in which they sorted their set of buttons. As students share, record each sort in equation form where everyone can see it. For example, if one of the sorts was seven buttons with four holes and three buttons with two holes, record *7 + 3 = 10* or *10 = 7 + 3*.

8. After each set of partners has shared, ask students to look at all the equations generated. Ask the following key questions. Emphasize to students that all the equations are different ways to make ten. No matter how each person sorted the buttons, he or she still has 10 buttons.

Key Questions

- What do you notice about the equations?
- How are the equations different?
- What is the same about all of the equations?

Extension

Going Beyond Buttons

Students will need many experiences with the concept that partitioning a set several ways does not change the quantity. Have students sort additional objects. Some ideas include nuts (in the shell), keys, pieces of fabric, nuts and bolts, and attribute blocks. Make sure the number in each set of objects to sort remains the same to demonstrate that the quantity remains unchanged.

FORMATIVE ASSESSMENT IN ACTION: QUESTIONS

Use these questions to help guide your observations of students as they are engaged in the lesson. Your focused observations in turn support the instructional decisions you'll make for individual students and your class.

- Does the student work well with his or her partner? What roles does each partner take on to complete the task?

- Is the student able to sort the buttons and classify them into different sets?

- How does the student represent his or her sorted sets of buttons?

- Does the student make the connection that both of the button sorts have 10 buttons?

STUDENTS WHO STRUGGLE

Helping Students Move beyond Using Pictures Only

Students will use a form of representation that makes sense to them. Sharing the range of forms of representation validates each as useful. Eventually, you want children to move beyond using pictures, only, to show their thinking. By "scaffolding" during the sharing process, students gain different perspectives on the possibilities for representing their mathematical understandings (see the rubric on page 128 as an example of a means to help you select student work when scaffolding during processing time). Having many opportunities for problem solving and processing time to share different ways to represent mathematical thinking is critical to helping students move beyond using pictures only. Some students will need to be encouraged to try someone else's way of representation.

WHAT HAPPENS IN MY CLASSROOM

When I am creating the sets of buttons, I keep in mind two things. First, I want to be certain all the sets have the same quantity of buttons. This allows students to recognize that all the equations have the same sum. Second, I quickly presort the buttons into sets. Some of the sets of buttons may have metal buttons, cloth-covered buttons, or buttons with shanks, but not all the sets will have buttons with these attributes. By presorting the buttons before I give the sets of 10 to students, the sharing process becomes more interesting; there is a greater variety of ways in which students classify the buttons.

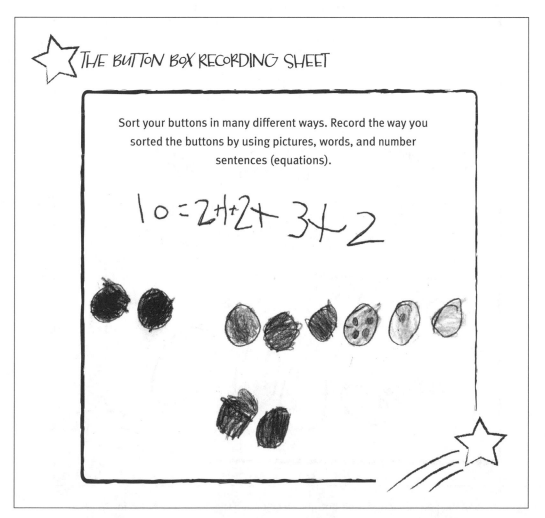

FIGURE 14 Jessica and her partner sorted their buttons by color for *The Button Box* lesson.

I keep the presorted buttons in separate plastic bags for future use, so I do not have to presort them every time I use them. Before storing them after the lesson, I double-check the number of buttons to ensure that all sets have the same quantity.

In my class there is always a variety of ways in which students represent their button sorts. Some partners represent only with pictures. Some partners use pictures and words, and still others use pictures, words, and numbers. I've even had students use pictures, words, numbers, and write an equation. (See Figures 14 and 15.)

FIGURE 15 Chris and his partner sorted their buttons by color and the number of holes for *The Button Box* lesson.

I try to have students share their work in the order just described, from least sophisticated to most sophisticated. This scaffolding during the sharing process validates everyone's thinking and gradually builds to the more abstract representation (see the rubric on page 128 as an example of a means to help you select student work when scaffolding during processing time). I also encourage students to try a representation they have not used before the next time we are solving a problem. I connect all the ways that the buttons were sorted to an equation, regardless of whether the partners created an equation. This allows me to make a connection to symbols that is directly related to a concrete experience students have had. I always emphasize that there are many ways to partition a quantity, but the quantity remains the same.

FORMATIVE ASSESSMENT IN ACTION: TEACHER AND STUDENT CHECKLISTS

The Button Box Teacher Checklist

Checklists are invaluable in helping to focus your observations as well as to document student behaviors, responses, and reactions to lessons. Each column in the checklist specifies what to observe while students are engaged in the mathematical activity. Having the checklist ready on a clipboard, and easily accessible, helps to ensure necessary documentation and recording takes place. For more on using teacher checklists as a successful formative assessment practice, see page 15.

The Button Box Student Checklist

This checklist helps students monitor their own learning, set math goals, and ultimately share academic progress with their parents. Each child should have his or her own student checklist and should keep it in his or her student notebook. For more on using student checklists (including video clips) as a successful formative assessment practice, see page 20.

TEACHER CHECKLIST: THE BUTTON BOX

Student Names and Date	Works Well with a Partner	Sorts Set in at Least Two Ways	Forms of Representation: Pictures, Words, Numbers, Equations	Understands Set Can Be Partitioned and Quantity Remains Constant	Notes

STUDENT CHECKLIST

THE BUTTON BOX

NAME _____

I work well with my partner.	I sort my set two different ways.	I represent my thinking using pictures, words, and numbers.	I know that the quantity does not change, no matter how I sort the set.

DATE _____ DATE _____

DATE _____ DATE _____

L-5 HIDE AND SNAKE

Related Lessons

Consider teaching first G-2 *Guess My Pattern*. Consider as a follow-up lesson P-3 *Growth Patterns*.

Overview

Hide and Snake by Keith Baker is a mosaic adventure that invites readers to trace a snake's movements as it slithers through yarn, hats, cats, and more. This bright, visually engaging book sets the context for students to create their own pattern-block snakes. After making their patterns, students use precut paper pattern blocks and white school glue to make a permanent record of their work. This lesson reinforces the concept of a repeating pattern as well as providing meaningful practice in recognizing, extending, and creating patterns.

Common Core State Standards

Aligned to the mathematical practices in the **Common Core State Standards**

Although pattern is not explicitly referenced in the Common Core State Standards, such experiences are pivotal in creating a foundation for number/repeated addition/multiplication.

Goals for Student Understanding

These goals are aligned to the mathematical practices in the Common Core State Standards. Students will

- Make sense of problems and persevere in solving them.
- Model with mathematics.
- Use appropriate tools strategically.
- Attend to precision.
- Look for and make use of structure.

Setting

Small group and individually

Time

Approximately thirty minutes

Materials

Hide and Snake by Keith Baker
pattern blocks for each student
precut paper pattern block shapes for each student
4-by-6 inch black construction paper, 1 for each student
white school glue
white crayons or silver marker
Hide and Snake Teacher Checklist
Hide and Snake Student Checklist, 1 copy per student

Key Vocabulary

pattern blocks
record
repeating pattern
shapes
unit

TEACHING DIRECTIONS

Part 1: Reading the Book

1. Gather students in the whole-group area of your classroom. Introduce and read the popular children's book *Hide and Snake*. As you read, pause for students to search for patterns in the illustrations. Ask students to share what they notice.

Part 2: Creating Pattern-Block Snakes and Recording Patterns

2. After reading the story, tell students that they will each create their own pattern out of pattern blocks. Ask students to choose at least two different pattern blocks to create their pattern. Model an example of a pattern-block snake using the blue rhombus and an orange square in an AB pattern.

3. Explain to students you are unable to save your pattern-block snake, so you will record the snake on black construction paper using paper pattern blocks and white school glue.

4. Talk through the process of recording the pattern on paper. "I am going to glue my first shape all the way on the left side of my paper. I am gluing my blue rhombus right next to my orange square side-by-side, edges touching but not overlapping." Then write your name on the corner of your paper using a white crayon or silver marker.

5. Ask students to think of a pattern that is different from yours (it would not be very interesting to have five snakes that looked the same!). Remind students that they have their own good ideas to record.

Part 3: Sharing Pattern-Block Snakes

6. When students finish recording their pattern-block snakes, gather everyone in the whole-group area of your classroom. Share each student's pattern block recording; point to each pattern block shape and ask the student to read his or her pattern with you. For example, "Blue, green, blue, green, blue, green." Ask the following key questions. Repeat this with the snakes that were made during this small-group/center time.

Key Question

- Is this a pattern? Why? Why not?

Extension

Showing Units in a Pattern

For this extension, students will need their recorded pattern-block snakes from the lesson, toothpicks, and white school glue. Students who demonstrate a deeper understanding of pattern and ability to record their work may be ready for a challenge. Ask the student to read his or her pattern to you. After the student reads his or her pattern, ask, "What is the unit, or the part that keeps repeating?" For example, if the pattern is triangle, square, triangle, square, triangle, square, the unit is triangle, square. The triangle, square is the part that keeps repeating. Ask the student to glue toothpicks on his or her recorded pattern to show each unit within the pattern. See samples of student work done in this extension in the "What Happens in My Classroom" section.

FORMATIVE ASSESSMENT IN ACTION: QUESTIONS

Use these questions to help guide your observations of students as they are engaged in the lesson. Your focused observations in turn support the instructional decisions you'll make for individual students and your class.

- Does the student recognize a repeating pattern? How does he or she describe the pattern?

- Can the student copy a repeating pattern?

- Can the student extend a repeating pattern?

- Is the student able to create his or her own repeating pattern? What type of pattern does he or she create? AB? ABBA? ABC?

- Does the student recognize the repeating unit within the pattern?

STUDENTS WHO STRUGGLE

Helping Students Who Are Not Creating a Repeating Pattern

Because this is an early experience, many children have difficulty creating their own repeating pattern. Often they connect many pattern blocks together that do not create a pattern. When this happens, ask the student who created the snake to "read" the pattern with you. Ask the student to then predict what would come next. Establish that the pattern-block snake he or she created is not a repeating pattern. Ask the student to choose only two different colors or shapes. Take several blocks of each chosen color out of the pattern-block container with the student. At this point, some children can create their own pattern using the limited selection of blocks. Some students may need support in starting the pattern. In this case, start the pattern as you talk about what you are doing. For example, "Okay, I am going to use a blue rhombus first; next, I will use a red trapezoid, then another blue rhombus. I am lining up my pattern blocks side-by-side so that the sides touch. What do you think will come next in this pattern?" Encourage the student to extend the pattern that you started.

Helping Students Who Are Experiencing Difficulty Recording Their Pattern

Students who have not had many experiences gluing paper pattern blocks onto paper can be uncertain where to begin gluing. When you model recording your pattern-block snake on paper, talk through what you are doing carefully and clearly. You may also notice students overlapping the paper pattern blocks as they are gluing, sometimes to the extent that their recorded pattern is hard to recognize. When this happens, ask the student to help you remove the glued paper pattern blocks that are overlapping. Refer back to the pattern that they created using the pattern blocks. Draw the student's attention to the placement of the pattern-block manipulatives; the blocks are placed side-by-side with the edges touching, but not overlapping. Ask the student to keep that in mind as he or she records the pattern on paper.

WHAT HAPPENS IN MY CLASSROOM

Hide and Snake is a teacher-directed center during our math time. This lesson takes place early in our study of pattern, following opportunities students have had to copy, extend, and create their own patterns. After all students have worked with me at the *Hide and Snake* center, I have the materials available for students to return to during a choice time. I continue to make this an option until I am satisfied with the progress of my students and while there is student interest (which is usually longer than I expect!). Students often choose to return and create more elaborate snakes with repeated experiences. (See Figure 16.) When necessary, I sit at the *Hide and Snake* table and invite students who do not choose to return, or students who need additional practice, to work with me. My presence at the table often convinces students to return who may not do so otherwise. I am also able to give specific support to students who need it.

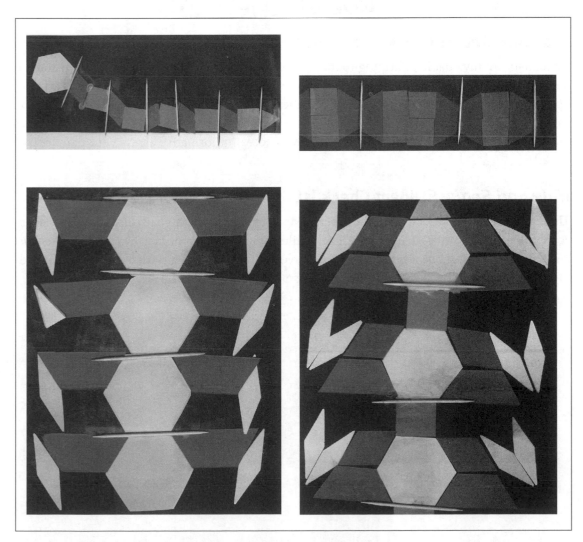

FIGURE 16 Students created snakes for the *Showing Units in a Pattern* extension

I use many paper pattern blocks throughout the school year. Paper pattern blocks can be time-consuming to make. I often ask parent volunteers and older student volunteers to make these pattern-block shapes. I use plastic bags to store sorted paper pattern-block shapes. For example, I have one bag for red trapezoids and one bag for green triangles. Recently, I found a small plastic container with six drawers. Now I use it to store the precut paper pattern blocks. I tape a paper pattern block to the outside of each drawer to distinguish which drawer holds which shape. This six-drawer container is out and accessible to students.

White crayons or silver markers are both useful to write students' names on the front corner of their work when it is on black paper. When displayed, having children's names visible on the front of student work makes it easier for parents to locate (and admire!) their child's creations.

FORMATIVE ASSESSMENT IN ACTION: TEACHER AND STUDENT CHECKLISTS

Hide and Snake Teacher Checklist

Checklists are invaluable in helping to focus your observations as well as to document student behaviors, responses, and reactions to lessons. Each column in the checklist specifies what to observe while students are engaged in the mathematical activity. Having the checklist ready on a clipboard, and easily accessible, helps to ensure necessary documentation and recording takes place. For more on using teacher checklists as a successful formative assessment practice, see page 15.

Hide and Snake Student Checklist

This checklist helps students monitor their own learning, set math goals, and ultimately share academic progress with their parents. Each child should have his or her own student checklist and should keep it in his or her student notebook. For more on using student checklists (including video clips) as a successful formative assessment practice, see page 20.

TEACHER CHECKLIST: HIDE AND SNAKE

Student Names and Date	Recognizes a Pattern	Extends a Pattern	Creates a Pattern	Records a Pattern	Knows Where the Unit Repeats	Notes

From *How to Assess While You Teach: Math: Formative Assessment Practices and Lessons, Grades K–2: A Multimedia Professional Learning Resource* by Dana Islas.
© 2011 Scholastic Inc. Permission granted to photocopy for nonprofit use in a classroom or similar place dedicated to face-to-face educational instruction.

STUDENT CHECKLIST

HIDE AND SNAKE

NAME _____

I recognize patterns.	I can extend a pattern.	I can create a pattern.	I can record my pattern.	I know where the unit repeats.

DATE _____

DATE _____

DATE _____

DATE _____

L-6 LOTTIE'S NEW BEACH TOWEL

Related Lessons

Consider as a follow-up lesson any lesson in the problem-solving section (P-1 through P-6).

Overview

The delightful adventures in *Lottie's New Beach Towel*, introduced to me by my colleague Chris Brunette inspire the problem solver in every student. In this story, Lottie receives a gift of a new beach towel from her aunt. She takes it along for a day at the beach with her friend Herbie. This day proves to be quite an adventure as she encounters many dilemmas. Lottie is thoughtful, resourceful, and a very good problem solver! Students take their turn at being problem solvers, and figure out how many seashells Lottie has when she returns home. In the final part of the lesson, students process their experience by describing the strategies they used to solve the problem.

Common Core State Standards

Operations and Algebraic Thinking: Standard K.OA

Understand addition as putting together and adding to, and understand subtraction as taking apart and taking from.

Operations and Algebraic Thinking: Standard 1.OA

Represent and solve problems involving addition and subtraction.

Add and subtract within 20.

Work with addition and subtraction equations.

Operations and Algebraic Thinking: Standard 2.OA

Represent and solve problems involving addition and subtraction.

Add and subtract within 20.

> Aligned to the mathematical practices in the **Common Core State Standards**

Goals for Student Understanding

These goals are aligned to the mathematical practices in the Common Core State Standards. Students will

- Make sense of problems and persevere in solving them.
- Reason abstractly and quantitatively.
- Construct viable arguments and critique the reasoning of others.
- Model with mathematics.
- Use appropriate tools strategically.
- Attend to precision.
- Look for and make use of structure.
- Look for and express regularity in repeated reasoning.

Setting

Whole group and small group

Time

Approximately twenty minutes

Materials

Lottie's New Beach Towel by Petra Mathers
Reproducible L: *Lottie's New Beach Towel*
  Recording Sheet, 1 copy per student
  (Version 1 or 2)

Problem-Solving Teacher Checklist
Problem-Solving Student Checklist, 1 copy
  per student

Key Vocabulary

persistent
problem solver
resourceful

TEACHING DIRECTIONS

Part 1: Making Predictions and Reading the Book

1. Gather students in the whole-group area of your classroom. Ask students to look at the cover of the book *Lottie's New Beach Towel* and make predictions about where the story might take place. Who is on the front cover? What is she doing?

2. Read the book *Lottie's New Beach Towel* to your students.

Part 2: What Makes a Good Problem Solver?

3. After reading the story, ask students to tell you the different problems Lottie encountered. How did Lottie handle the dilemmas she faced?

4. Emphasize to students that Lottie was very thoughtful and resourceful. Lottie did not give up; she was persistent. Ask students to think about how they can be resourceful and persistent as they solve problems during math time.

Part 3: Problem Solving with Lottie

5. Reread the book to your students. This time, tell them you have a problem that you would like them to help you solve. Tell students they can use counters, pictures, words, numbers, and equations to represent their thinking. After everyone has a chance to solve the problem, strategies will be shared as a class.

6. Introduce students to one version of Reproducible L: *Lottie's New Beach Towel* Recording Sheet (note that there are two versions: one is a separate/result unknown; the other is a separate/start unknown). Read the problem at the top of the recording sheet several times. Ask several volunteers to restate the problem. When it seems that students clearly know what the problem is to be solved, give them each a copy of the recording sheet and have them work in small groups at their tables.

7. Circulate as students are working. Remind them that you want them to represent their thinking on paper to share with others. Assist students who need clarification and note those strategies you want to share with the whole class.

8. As students finish, ask them to place their recording sheets in a designated place. Have each student do an independent task until others have a chance to finish.

Part 4: Processing the Problem

9. Think back on your observations while students were completing their recording sheets. Who solved the problem accurately? What strategy was used? Select a few pieces of student work to share with the whole class.

10. Gather students in the whole-group area of your classroom. Organize the strategies shared; begin with a simple, yet accurate representation and build up to more sophisticated strategies (see the student work examples in the "What Happens in My Classroom" section of this lesson). Talk about what strategies were used to represent mathematical thinking (drawing pictures, writing numbers, showing organization, using counters, and so on). If students are comfortable sharing in the whole group, have them describe their own work. Hold each student's paper for everyone to see while he or she communicates the strategies used to the whole group.

Extension

Using Different Contexts

Pose mathematically similar problems in a different context to give students an opportunity to use some of the strategies shared during the processing time. Two versions of Reproducible L have been provided for this purpose. Offering different types of word problems for students to solve helps them to develop a stronger understanding of what addition and subtraction actually mean. It is very common to find "join" and "change" problems for young students to solve written in textbooks and by teachers. By providing opportunities for students to grapple with word problems with varying structures, they will build a foundation for their mathematical work in the upper grades. For more on using different contexts, see "Repeated Experiences" in the introduction to problem-solving lessons on page 128.

FORMATIVE ASSESSMENT IN ACTION: QUESTIONS

Use these questions to help guide your observations of students as they are engaged in the lesson. Your focused observations in turn support the instructional decisions you'll make for individual students and your class.

- Does the student understand the problem?

- Does the student solve the problem in more than one way?

- How does the student represent his or her mathematical thinking? Counters (physical model), pictures, words, numbers, equations?

- Is the student able to communicate his or her ideas to others? Which setting is the student able to share in? Partners, small group, whole group?

TEACHING TIP: RESTATING THE PROBLEM

Asking students to restate the problem helps make everyone aware of the problem. This is useful to many children, especially those who are not able to read the problem at the top of the recording sheet yet.

TEACHING TIP: AS STUDENTS FINISH

As students finish their work, ask them either to read a book or work on a flat pattern-block design. Both of these tasks are flexible and offer students choices. Students may work alone or with a partner, they may choose the book they want to read, or they may determine what they will create with pattern blocks. Both books and pattern blocks can be cleaned up quickly after everyone has finished the lesson's work and is ready to proceed to the next part of the lesson.

TEACHING TIP: SELECTING STUDENT STRATEGIES TO SHARE

Be mindful about selecting strategies and students to share their strategies. There are often several students who are able to represent a particular strategy through their work. Share accurate, useful strategies while varying the students who are selected to share. Use the rubric on page 128 to help determine how to select student work when scaffolding during processing time with problem-solving lessons.

STUDENTS WHO STRUGGLE

Helping Students Who Are Not Yet Ready to Speak in Front of the Whole Group

Some students may not yet be comfortable sharing their work in front of the whole group. If this is the case, ask the student to come up and hold his or her paper while you describe their work. This involves the student in the sharing process, even if he or she isn't talking. Plus, it lets everyone see the work (note that, often, when a student holds his or her paper, he or she will have the paper facing toward him- or herself, rather than the group; point out that everyone needs to be able to see what is on the paper). As the student holds his or her paper, I also use this opportunity to model how to share mathematical strategies. I gradually shift from talking about the student's work to having the student talk about his or her mathematical strategies.

WHAT HAPPENS IN MY CLASSROOM

When a strategy to represent mathematical thinking, such as drawing pictures, is shared, I say to the whole group, "Raise your hand if you used pictures to solve the problem." I repeat this process for each strategy shared. I do not ask each child to come up to talk about his or her work, but I do validate useful strategies and recognize all students who are using them. The following are some of the strategies students have recorded in my classroom. (See Figures 17 through 22.)

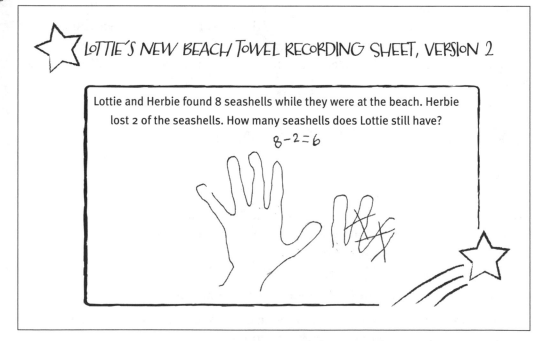

FIGURE 17 Emily used her fingers to show her thinking in solving the problem for the *Lottie's New Beach Towel* lesson.

FIGURE 18 Breiann used cubes to show her thinking in solving the problem for the *Lottie's New Beach Towel* lesson.

FIGURE 19 Jamie used a ten-frame to show her thinking in solving the problem for the *Lottie's New Beach Towel* lesson.

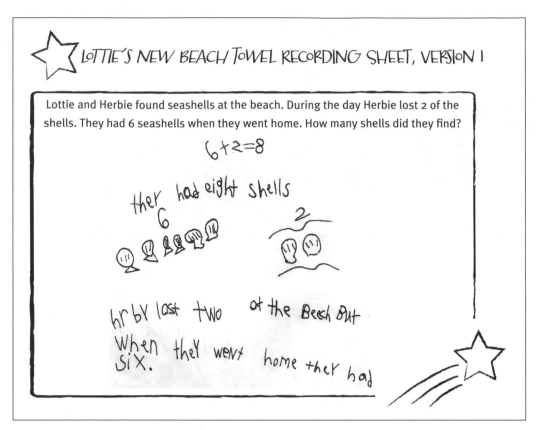

FIGURE 20 Arissa used pictures, words, and numbers to show her thinking in solving the problem for the *Lottie's New Beach Towel* lesson.

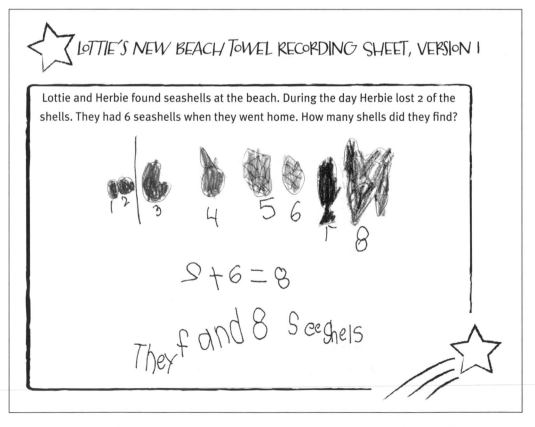

FIGURE 21 Isayol used the strategy counting on to solve the problem for the *Lottie's New Beach Towel* lesson.

FIGURE 22 Cecil recorded the use of manipulatives to solve the problem for the *Lottie's New Beach Towel* lesson.

Formative Assessment in Action: Teacher and Student Checklists

For this lesson, use the Problem-Solving Teacher Checklist and the Problem-Solving Student Checklist on pages 137 and 138.

FORMATIVE ASSESSMENT THROUGH PROBLEM SOLVING

In the Common Core State Standards, the first mathematical practice listed and emphasized for kindergarten through grade 2 is problem solving—specifically, students need to "make sense of problems and persevere in solving them." Problem-solving lessons are crucial to helping students apply what they know and represent their thinking in a way that makes sense to them. The problem-solving lessons featured in this section form a natural extension to the games and literature lessons previously introduced. Like the previous lessons, they were created through a process of formative assessment in my classroom. Each lesson supports implementation of the seven key formative assessment practices while simultaneously emphasizing mathematical thinking. The following are some of the experiences and insights I've learned in successfully implementing problem-solving-focused mathematical lessons.

One of the first steps I take in a problem-solving lesson is to establish, with all my students in a whole group, how to share their mathematical thinking. I ask students, "What are some of the ways you can represent your mathematical thinking?"

Whole-Group Setting

To start with, I recommend a whole-group setting for problem solving with students. Whole-group settings allow everyone in the classroom community to have a common experience. In addition, many more strategies come from an entire group of students, creating a richer sharing and learning process. For more on the importance of whole-group settings, see Section I, page 3.

Thinking of Strategies

One of the first steps I take in a problem-solving lesson is to establish, with all my students in a whole group, how to share their mathematical thinking. I ask students, "What are some of the ways you can represent your mathematical thinking?" I pose this question then generate a list of ideas with the students for everyone to see. Some of the ideas I look for are pictures, words, numbers, equations, manipulatives (physical model), and more than one way to solve the problem. I can refer to this list as needed to remind students what they can use to solve a problem.

Introducing the Problem

Introducing the problem clearly and carefully is important to students' success in solving the problem. When introducing a problem-solving lesson, I read the problem to students several times. Afterward, I ask several students to restate the problem using their own words. After many students repeat the problem, I pass out the corresponding recording sheet. Each of the following lessons has a reproducible recording sheet for students to record their thinking. The problem is always at the top of the sheet; the rest of the sheet is intentionally left blank for students to represent their thinking.

Solving the Problem

Students work on the problem in small groups, partners, or individually at tables. I let the students know what the grouping will be for the problem before the recording sheet is passed out to them. With every problem that I pose, I want to know how students will apply their prior knowledge and experiences to the situation. How will they approach the problem? What makes sense to students at this time to solve a problem? What tools will they use? How will they represent their thinking on paper? Can they share their thinking with others?

Processing the Problem: Selecting and Sharing Students' Strategies

I have several objectives while students are working. First, I am available to provide support and to make necessary clarifications. I try to get another student to clarify before I step in, asking questions like, "Who can remind me what the problem was?" Second, I want to determine who I will ask to share their thinking when we return to a whole-group setting (the processing part of the lesson). To do this, I need to observe students carefully and take notes as appropriate. Third, I want to determine the order in which I will have students share.

It's important to share strategies in a structured order. When students reconvene as a whole group to process their experience, I begin the discussion by sharing a student's thinking that is a simple yet accurate way to solve the problem. Each strategy I share thereafter progresses in sophistication. This organization in presenting strategies helps students see how each strategy is connected and related, without becoming overwhelmed.

Looking at Student Work with a Rubric

Use the following rubric to help determine how to select student work when "scaffolding" during processing time with problem-solving lessons.

TEACHING TIP: USING MANIPULATIVES

Students always have access to math manipulatives, ten-frames, and number lines in my classroom. Even though I remind students that they may use anything they find helpful to solve the problem, I place manipulatives on each table to encourage students' use of them. Some manipulatives are more useful than others to solve problems. For example, two-color counters provide a valuable physical model when exploring combinations of a number, because a group of five two-color counters can be turned over strategically, one by one, to show combinations (four red and one yellow, three red and two yellow, and so forth). The two-color counters are also part of the students' experience from prior lessons such as *Shake and Spill Combinations*. Although cubes or rods might also be used, they may not be as easy to represent one's mathematical thinking for this context.

Rubric for Scaffolding Student Work Prior to Processing Time

Found no solution	Used pictures that coincide with problem to represent thinking	Used numbers to represent thinking	Used multiple representation (pictures, words, numbers, manipulatives, etc.)
0	1	2	3
Drew pictures unrelated to problem	Pictures are randomly drawn	Numbers used demonstrate an understanding of problem	Used a mathematical tool (T-chart, ten-frame, number line, hundreds chart)
0	1	2	3
Needed constant prompting from teacher	Pictures are organized	Wrote equations	Demonstrates a systematic way of thinking while using mathematical tools or representations
0	1	2	3

I always emphasize to students that there are many different paths to take to arrive at a solution. I refer back to the initial list of strategies we created at the start of the lesson; I write down additional ways that students solved the problem. I use bullets and keep the text simple. Afterward, I post examples of student work next to each bullet. A bullet might read, *Drew pictures*. Another bullet might read, *Used numbers*.

Repeated Experiences

Although a lesson might be over, on another day I may repeat the same type of problem within a different context. I pose many problems with the focus on combinations of a number. For example, I ask students to solve a combination problem such as the *Ants* problem (see lesson P-2). I then ask students to solve the other combination problem (the *Grapes* problem, also part of lesson P-2), within the next couple of days. As another example, I pose many problems with the focus on growth patterns. Besides including a variety of contexts, these problems should increase by different amounts, with different amounts of stages in the pattern. Examples of contexts with a growth pattern increasing by two are as follows: How many eyes are there in your committee or group? How many wheels do five bicycles have? How many eyes are there in our classroom? Some students approach growth-pattern problems via drawing pictures and counting all. Some students begin to see the growth patterns as repeated addition.

Repeating lessons within new contexts gives students who found one solution a chance to find more solutions next time, or students who were introduced to certain strategies during processing time have a chance to "try out" these strategies (or try entirely new ones!). On the other hand, a student who found more than one solution may try a way to become more organized and systematic (to be certain he or she found all the solutions). This student might use a T-chart to organize combinations, or two-color counters to make a physical model. Repeated experiences allow even the youngest students to own their ideas and to represent their thinking in different ways.

The Lessons

The following is a brief overview of each problem-solving lesson included in this section.

P-1 *How Many Frogs?,* page 130: This lesson picks up where L-2 *Five Little Speckled Frogs* left off, encouraging students to think about the jumping frogs in a problem-solving situation.

P-2 *Combinations of Ants and Grapes,* page 139: This lesson presents two problems—one involving digging for ants and the other, sharing grapes. The problems provide an opportunity for students to revisit the idea of combinations. Each problem is open-ended, having more than one solution.

P-3 *Growth Patterns,* page 145 ⊙ The two growth-pattern problems in this lesson are based on two popular children's books: *Comet's Nine Lives* and *See How They Grow: Butterflies.* The lesson encourages children to extend their experiences with repeating patterns in colors, shapes, words, and number.

P-4 *My Name in Color Tiles!,* page 152 ⊙ During this lesson, students use color tiles to create the letters in their first names. Their name "masterpieces" become the center of a mathematical task: writing equations that represent the combination of tiles in each letter.

P-5 *The Four-Triangle Problem,* page 160 This lesson extends students' work in geometry. Students put four triangles together to create different shapes. They then convene as a whole group and post their shapes in polygon categories.

P-6 *Students Write the Context,* page 167 ⊙ During this lesson, students write the story to an equation (the context for the problem). The lesson incorporates writing with math and provides insight to students' creative thinking.

> *A Note about L-6 Lottie's New Beach Towel: You'll find the lesson* Lottie's New Beach Towel *in the math and literature section of this resource (page 119); however, it's helpful to integrate Lottie into your problem-solving lessons, too. In the children's book* Lottie's New Beach Towel, *Lottie is very resourceful and she is a great problem solver. She persists through each obstacle she encounters. I want students to relate to Lottie in all they do. Be a problem solver! I read this book to children early during the school year to send them this message. I reread the book to students for enjoyment and as a reminder of what a problem solver might do when faced with a dilemma. I often hear students tell one another that they are like Lottie or "Don't say 'I can't.' Try like Lottie!"*

P-I HOW MANY FROGS?

Related Lessons

Consider teaching first G-3 *Building Quantities on a Ten-Frame*, G-4 *+1, –1 on a Ten-Frame*, and L-2 *Five Little Speckled Frogs*.

Overview

This lesson picks up where L-2 *Five Little Speckled Frogs* left off, encouraging students to think about the frogs in a separate problem-solving situation. This is a great opportunity for students to apply what they have learned about subtraction through previous lessons. It's also a wonderful way for the teacher to learn about strategies and models students are using to represent their mathematical thinking.

Common Core State Standards

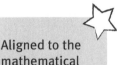
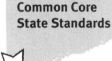

Aligned to the mathematical practices in the **Common Core State Standards**

Operations and Algebraic Thinking: Standard K.OA

Understand addition as putting together and adding to, and understand subtraction as taking apart and taking from.

Operations and Algebraic Thinking: Standard 1.OA

Represent and solve problems involving addition and subtraction.

Understand and apply properties of operations and the relationship between addition and subtraction.

Add and subtract within 20.

Work with addition and subtraction equations.

Operations and Algebraic Thinking: Standard 2.OA

Represent and solve problems involving addition and subtraction.

Add and subtract within 20.

Number and Operations in Base Ten: Standard 2.NBT

Use place value understanding and properties of operations to add and subtract.

Goals for Student Understanding

These goals are aligned to the mathematical practices in the Common Core State Standards. Students will

- Make sense of problems and persevere in solving them.
- Reason abstractly and quantitatively.
- Construct viable arguments and critique the reasoning of others.
- Model with mathematics.

- Use appropriate tools strategically.
- Attend to precision.

Setting

Whole group

Time

Approximately thirty to forty-five minutes

Materials

Five Little Speckled Frogs by Nikki Smith a variety of manipulatives (ten-frames, counters, and so on) on each table

Reproducible M: *How Many Frogs?* Recording Sheet, 1 copy for each student (version 1 or 2)
Problem-Solving Teacher Checklist
Problem-Solving Student Checklist, 1 copy per student

Key Vocabulary

communicate
model
represent
strategy

TEACHING DIRECTIONS

Part 1: Introducing the Problem

1. Gather students in the whole-group area of your classroom. Read the familiar book *Five Little Speckled Frogs*. Tell students you have a problem, related to the five little frogs, that you would like them to help you solve. Students can use counters, pictures, words, numbers, and equations to represent their thinking. After everyone has a chance to solve the problem, some strategies will be shared with the whole class.

2. Introduce students to Reproducible M: *How Many Frogs?* Recording Sheet (version 1 or 2). Read the problem at the top of the recording sheet several times. Ask several volunteers to restate the problem. When it seems that students clearly know what the problem is to be solved, give them each a copy of the recording sheet and have them work in small groups at their tables.

Part 2: Solving the Problem

3. Circulate as students are working. Take note of the strategies students are using that you want to share with the whole class. Remind students that you want them to represent their thinking on paper to share with others. Assist students needing clarification by asking, "Who can tell me what the problem is?" Not only does this question serve as a reminder, but it helps students stay focused on solving the problem posed (rather than a misinterpretation of the problem). Assist students having difficulty getting started by asking, "How could you represent the frogs?"

4. As students finish, ask them to place their recording sheets in a designated place. Have each student do an independent task until others have a chance to finish.

> **TEACHING TIP: RESTATING THE PROBLEM**
>
> Asking students to restate the problem helps make everyone aware of the problem. This is helpful to many children, especially English learners and those who are not able to read the problem at the top of the page yet.

Part 3: Processing the Problem

5. Think back on your observations while students were completing their recording sheets. Who solved the problem accurately? What strategy was used? Select a few pieces of student work to share with the whole class.

6. Gather students in the whole-group area of your classroom. Scaffold the strategies shared; begin with a simple, yet accurate representation and build up to more sophisticated strategies (for a rubric, see page 128). Talk about what strategies were used to represent mathematical thinking (drawing pictures, writing numbers, showing organization, using counters, and so forth).

> ### Strategies to Emphasize for How Many Frogs?
>
> - Uses pictures, words, numbers (with or without equation)
> - Counts back
> - Models using a ten-frame
> - Uses a number line

If students are comfortable sharing in the whole group, have them describe their own work. Hold each student's paper for everyone to see while he or she communicates the strategies used to the whole group.

Extension

Using Different Contexts

Pose mathematically similar problems in a different context to give students an opportunity to use some of the strategies shared during the processing time. Two versions of Reproducible M have been provided for this purpose. Offering different types of word problems for students to solve helps them to develop a stronger understanding of what addition and subtraction actually mean. You can commonly find "join" and "change" problems for young students to solve. By providing opportunities for students to grapple with word problems with varying structures, they will build a foundation for their mathematical work in the upper grades. For more on using different contexts, see "Repeated Experiences" in the introduction to problem-solving lessons, page 126.

FORMATIVE ASSESSMENT IN ACTION: QUESTIONS

Use these questions to help guide your observations of students as they are engaged in the lesson. Your focused observations in turn support the instructional decisions you'll make for individual students and your class.

- Does the student understand the problem?
- Does the student solve the problem in more than one way?
- How does the student represent his or her mathematical thinking? Counters (physical model), pictures, ten-frame, words, numbers, equations, or a combination of ways?

- Is the student able to communicate his or her ideas to others? Which setting is the student able to share in? Partners, small group, whole group?

STUDENTS WHO STRUGGLE

Helping Students Who Are Not Yet Ready to Speak in Front of the Whole Group

Some students may not yet be comfortable sharing their work in front of the hold group. If this is the case, ask the student to come up and hold his or her paper while you describe their work. This involves the student in the sharing process, even if he or she isn't talking. Plus, it lets everyone see the work (note that often when a student holds his or her paper, he or she will have the paper facing toward him- or herself, rather than the group; point out that everyone needs to be able to see what is on the paper). As the student holds his or her paper, also use this opportunity to model how to share mathematical strategies. Gradually shift from talking about the student's work to having the student talk about his or her mathematical strategies.

WHAT HAPPENS IN MY CLASSROOM

Early in our problem-solving processing time during the year, I ask a student to come up and hold his or her work while I describe their strategies. I model how I want students to share their work by making statements such as, "Faith used drawings to represent the frogs in the problem. Her drawings are organized because she put them in a line." I want our processing time to shift from me describing the student work to the students sharing what they did to represent and show thinking.

During processing time, after a strategy to represent mathematical thinking (such as drawing pictures) is shared, I say to the whole group, "Raise your hand if you used pictures to solve the problem." I repeat this process for each strategy shared. I do not ask each child to come up to talk about his or her work, but I do validate useful strategies and recognize all students who are using them. The following are some of the strategies students have recorded in my classroom. I asked students to share work in the order presented here during our processing time.

Student Strategies

Isabella used multiple forms of representation (organized pictures, words, and numbers) to share her thinking, so I shared her work with the whole group first, hoping that all students would be able to identify with at least one of the strategies. I asked Carlos to share his work second because he drew the ten-frame neatly for others to see and understand. Isayah was the only student to use a number line to solve this problem; I pointed this out next. I wanted Isayah's strategy to be shared to encourage other students to try it for themselves in subsequent problem-solving situations. I chose Aliyah's work to be shared after these because she included an equation in her representation. (See Figures 23 through 27.)

TEACHING TIP: SELECTING STUDENT STRATEGIES TO SHARE

Be mindful about selecting strategies and students to share their strategies. There are often several students who are able to represent a particular strategy through their work. Share accurate, useful strategies while varying the students who are selected to share. Use the rubric on page 128 to help determine how to select student work when "scaffolding" during processing time with problem-solving lessons.

FIGURE 23 *How Many Frogs?* Isabella's recording sheet. Isabella demonstrated her ability to use several ways to express her thinking. She used pictures to represent the total group of seven frogs, including two jumping into the water and five remaining on the log. She wrote words and numbers to show her thinking: *2 jumped in the water and there were 5 more.*

FIGURE 24 *How Many Frogs?* Carlos's recording sheet. Carlos used a familiar mathematical tool to solve this problem. To share his process with others, he drew a ten-frame—the math tool that made sense to him—to show his thinking in solving the problem.

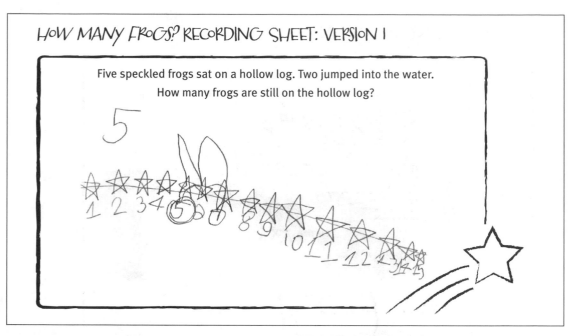

FIGURE 25 Isayah solved the problem using a number line—the math tool that made sense to him—to show his thinking in solving the problem.

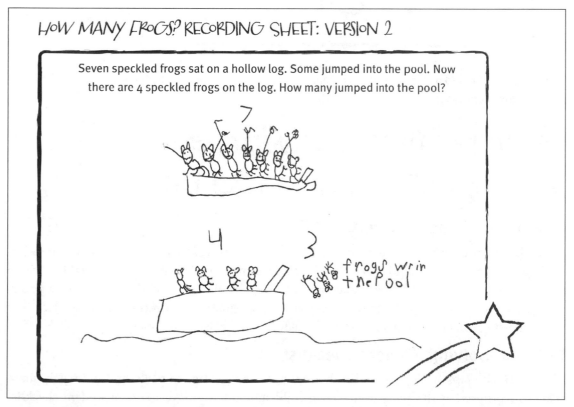

FIGURE 26 Evan used pictures to show before and after the frogs jumped and also used scenarios, words, and numbers to show his thinking. He wrote: *3 frogs were in the pool.*

FIGURE 27 Aliyah used pictures, an equation, and a number sentence to show her thinking in solving the problem *How Many Frogs?*

Formative Assessment in Action: Teacher and Student Checklists

Problem-Solving Teacher Checklist

Checklists are invaluable in helping to focus your observations as well as to document student behaviors, responses, and reactions to lessons. Each column in the checklist specifies what to observe while students are engaged in the mathematical activity. Having the checklist ready on a clipboard, and easily accessible, helps to ensure necessary documentation and recording takes place. For more on using teacher checklists as a successful formative assessment practice, see page 15.

Problem-Solving Student Checklist

This checklist helps students monitor their own learning, set math goals, and ultimately share academic progress with their parents. Each child should have his or her own student checklist and should keep it in his or her student notebook. For more on using student checklists (including video clips) as a successful formative assessment practice, see page 20.

PROBLEM-SOLVING TEACHER CHECKLIST: HOW MANY FROGS

Student Names and Date	Draws Pictures	Uses Organiza-tion: Drawings, Numbers Are Lined Up	Uses Multiple Repre-sentations (Pictures, Words, Numbers, Physical Model)	Uses Mathematical Tools (Ten-Frame, Hundreds Chart, Number Line, T-Chart)	Uses a Systematic Way to Demonstrate Thinking	Shares Work During Processing Time	Notes

STUDENT CHECKLIST

NAME _____

HOW MANY FROGS?

I used pictures.	I used words.	I used numbers.	I am organized.	I used mathematical tools.	I shared my work with others.

DATE _____

DATE _____

DATE _____

DATE _____

P-2 COMBINATIONS OF ANTS AND GRAPES

Related Lessons

Consider teaching first G-5 *Practicing Combinations* and G-6 *Shake and Spill Combinations*.

Overview

This lesson presents two problem-solving contexts for students to apply what they have learned about combinations of a number—one involving digging for ants and the other, sharing grapes. The problems provide an opportunity for students to explore, practice, represent, and record their understanding of combinations. Each problem is open-ended, having more than one solution. This is a great opportunity for the teacher to learn about students' level of understanding of combinations and the strategies and models students are using to represent their mathematical thinking.

> Aligned to the mathematical practices in the **Common Core State Standards**

Common Core State Standards

Counting and Cardinality: Standard K.CC

Know number names and the count sequence.

Operations and Algebraic Thinking: Standard K.OA

Understand addition is putting together and adding to, and understand subtraction as taking apart and taking from.

Operations and Algebraic Thinking: Standard 1.OA

Represent and solve problems involving addition and subtraction.

Operations and Algebraic Thinking: Standard 2.OA

Add and subtract within 20.

> **TEACHING TIP: STANDARD 2.OA**
>
> The correlating second-grade Common Core State Standard is listed. In order for this lesson to meet this standard, the numbers in the problem need to be adjusted.

Goals for Student Understanding

These goals are aligned to the mathematical practices in the Common Core State Standards. Students will

• Make sense of problems and persevere in solving them.

• Reason abstractly and quantitatively.

• Construct viable arguments and critique the reasoning of others.

• Model with mathematics.

• Use appropriate tools strategically.

- Attend to precision.
- Look for and make use of structure.
- Look for and express regularity in repeated reasoning.

TEACHING TIP: ADJUSTING THE PROBLEM

Ask students to solve combinations problems based on the number your class is exploring. For example, if most of the students are working on combinations of five, then plug five in as the amount of ants or grapes. There will probably be students that are working with combinations of a number higher or lower than the majority of the students. In this case, simply change the number in the problem to meet the needs of the students. During processing time, share the different numbers being explored. Sharing the combinations for a smaller number can be a way to revisit ideas, whereas sharing the combinations for a larger number can motivate students; it gives a glimpse of what everyone will eventually be working on.

Setting

Whole group

Time

Approximately forty-five minutes

Materials

Reproducible N: *Combinations of Ants* Recording Sheet or Reproducible O: *Combinations of Grapes* Recording Sheet, 1 copy per student

a variety of counters, including two-color counters, on each table

Problem-Solving Teacher Checklist

Problem-Solving Student Checklist, 1 copy per student

Key Vocabulary

combinations

communicate

model

represent

strategy

TEACHING DIRECTIONS

For this lesson, follow the same directions as stated in P-1 *How Many Frogs?* For the recording sheet, use Reproducible N: *Combinations of Ants* or Reproducible O: *Combinations of Grapes*. When selecting student work to share during processing time, keep the following strategies in mind.

Strategies to Emphasize in Combinations Problems

- Represents with pictures, words, numbers (with and without equations)
- Organizes
- Uses a physical model (two-color counters work well for this type of problem)
- Uses lists (systematic thinking)
- Uses T-charts (systematic thinking)

WHAT HAPPENS IN MY CLASSROOM

During processing time, when a strategy to represent mathematical thinking, such as drawing pictures, is shared, I say to the whole group, "Raise your hand if you used pictures to solve the problem." I repeat this process for each strategy shared. I do not ask each child to come up to talk about his or her work, but I do validate useful strategies and recognize all students who are using them. The following are two sets of some of the strategies students have recorded in my classroom.

TEACHING TIP:
RUBRIC FOR
SELECTING
STUDENT WORK
TO SHARE

Use the rubric on page 128 to help you select student work when scaffolding during processing time.

Set 1: Student Strategies

I asked Ayak to share her work first, because she used drawings and an equation to represent her thinking and solution. Many students had work that looked similar to Jamie's. I chose to have Vance share his work last, because his equations were abstract, yet they could be connected to the drawings and equations that other students made to solve this problem. (See Figures 28 and 29.)

Set 2: Student Strategies

Thomas shared his solution first. It is very common for students to solve combinations problems focusing on an even number by using the double (for example, $5 + 5 = 10$). Most students were able to relate to this in Thomas's work, and I wanted this solution validated, because it is accurate. Also, Thomas made clear drawings and statements to represent his thinking. He seemed very much aware that his work would be seen by an audience. Isaiah's explanations are not as thorough as Thomas's; however, Isaiah did persist and he found three different possibilities to solve this problem. Fabian incorporated a T-chart to organize some of his possibilities. Mori's work was shared last because of its sophistication; she used multiple representations and demonstrated that she searched for many possibilities systematically. (See Figures 30 through 33.)

FIGURE 28 Jamie used an organized drawing with color coding and an equation, $4 + 2 = 6$, to show her thinking in solving the *Combinations of Ants* problem.

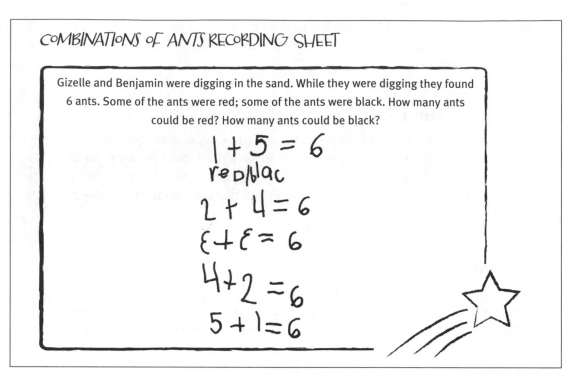

FIGURE 29 Vance used equations in a systematic approach to show his thinking in solving the *Combinations of Ants* problem.

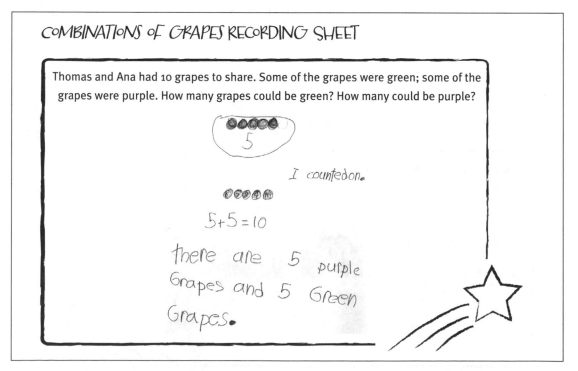

FIGURE 30 Thomas used a double to show his thinking in solving the *Combinations of Grapes* problem. His drawings indicate use of the counting-on strategy. He labeled and circled a set of five grapes, then labeled the other grapes 6, 7, 8, 9, 10. Tomas's writing complements and clarifies his understanding.

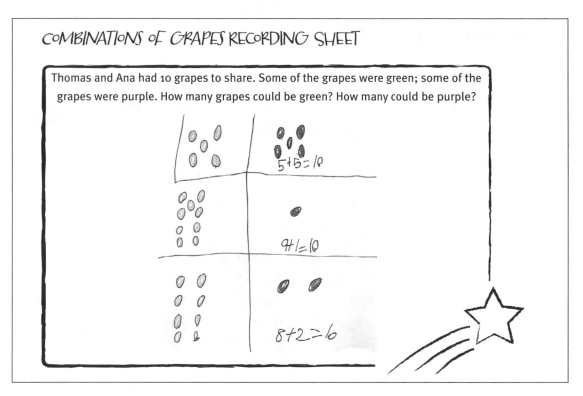

FIGURE 31 Isaiah found multiple solutions using an organized approach to show his thinking in solving the *Combinations of Grapes* problem. He wrote equations to correspond to each drawing.

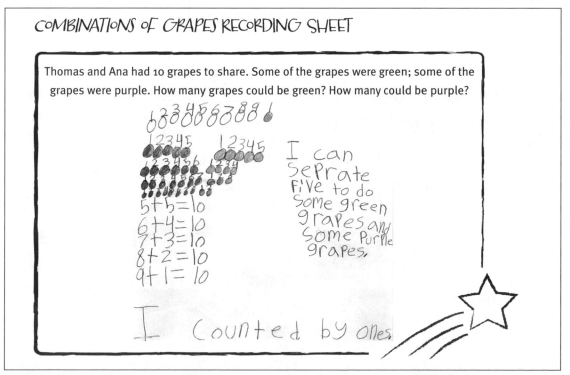

FIGURE 32 Fabian used a mathematical tool, a T-chart, to show his thinking in solving the *Combinations of Grapes* problem.

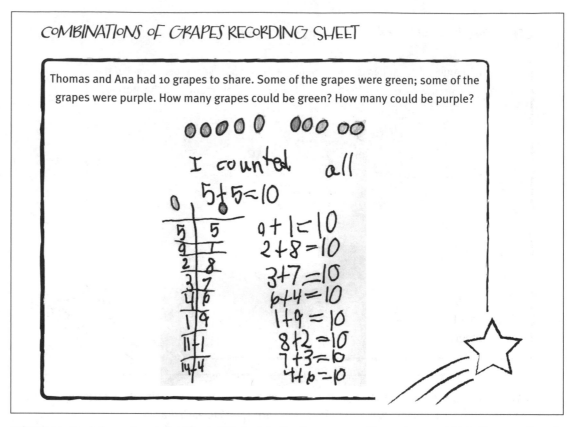

FIGURE 33 Mori showed organizational skills by labeling the grapes with numbers and including equations in her representations. She used a systematic approach as she created her drawings to find multiple solutions.

FORMATIVE ASSESSMENT IN ACTION: TEACHER AND STUDENT CHECKLISTS

For this lesson, use the Problem-Solving Teacher Checklist and Problem-Solving Student Checklist, pages 137 and 138.

P-3 GROWTH PATTERNS

Related Lessons

Consider teaching first G-2 *Guess My Pattern* and L-5 *Hide and Snake*.

Overview

The two growth-pattern problems in this lesson are based on two popular children's books: *Comet's Nine Lives* and *See How They Grow: Butterflies*. In *Comet's Nine Lives*, Comet the cat goes on a few adventures that quickly take eight of his nine lives. He discovers a more settled way to spend his ninth life. In *See How They Grow: Butterflies*, the life cycle of a butterfly unfolds through beautiful photographs and a simple, yet informative text. Both books are used as a springboard in this lesson to encourage children to extend their foundational experiences of repeating patterns with colors, shapes, and words to a repeating pattern in number. This is a great opportunity for the teacher to learn about strategies and models students are using to represent their mathematical thinking.

Common Core State Standards

Aligned to the mathematical practices in the **Common Core State Standards**

Counting and Cardinality: Standard K.CC

Count to tell number of objects.

Operations and Algebraic Thinking: Standard K.OA

Understand addition as putting together and adding to, and understand subtraction as taking apart and taking from.

Operations and Algebraic Thinking: Standard 1.OA

Represent and solve problems involving addition and subtraction.

Add and subtract within 20.

Work with addition and subtraction equations.

Operations and Algebraic Thinking: Standard 2.OA

Work with equal groups of objects to gain foundations for multiplication.

Goals for Student Understanding

These goals are aligned to the mathematical practices in the Common Core State Standards. Students will

- Make sense of problems and persevere in solving them.
- Reason abstractly and quantitatively.
- Construct viable arguments and critique the reasoning of others.
- Model with mathematics.

- Use appropriate tools strategically.
- Attend to precision.
- Look for and make use of structure.
- Look for and express regularity in repeated reasoning.

Setting

Whole group

Time

Approximately forty-five minutes

Materials

Comet's Nine Lives by Jan Brett
See How They Grow: Butterflies by
   Mary Ling
Reproducible P: *Growth Patterns:*
Comet's Nine Lives Recording Sheet
or Reproducible Q: *Growth Patterns:*

Butterflies Recording Sheet, 1 copy per
   student
a variety of counters at each table
Problem-Solving Teacher Checklist
Problem-Solving Student Checklist,
   1 copy per student

Key Vocabulary

communicate
model
repeating pattern
represent
strategy

TEACHING DIRECTIONS

Each of the two problems in this lesson connects nicely to a children's book. Follow the same directions as stated in P-1 *How Many Frogs?*, except first read the corresponding children's book (either *Comet's Nine Lives* or *See How They Grow: Butterflies*) to provide context and generate interest. When students are ready to solve the problem, use the appropriate recording sheet, either Reproducible P: *Growth Patterns:* Comet's Nine Lives Recording Sheet or Reproducible Q: *Growth Patterns:* Butterflies Recording Sheet. Note that *Comet's Nine Lives* is a more challenging version, because the numbers are larger; students are expected to increase by nine for each stage of the pattern. When selecting student work to share during processing time, keep the following strategies in mind.

Strategies to Emphasize in Growth Problems

- Uses pictures, words, and numbers to represent thinking
- Counts all
- Counts on
- Repeats addition
- Uses multiplicative thinking and reasoning

WHAT HAPPENS IN MY CLASSROOM

GROWTH PATTERNS

VIDEO CLIP K

In this clip, Dana discusses the three critical parts of a problem-solving lesson: introducing, solving, and processing the problem. The clip then focuses on the problem *Comet's Nine Lives* and takes viewers into Dana's classroom for a look at first-graders working together to complete the first two parts of the problem-solving lesson (to see part 3, processing the problem, watch the video clips in P-4 *My Name in Color Tiles!* and P-6 *Students Write the Context*). *As you watch the clip, consider:*

- What expectations are part of this classroom's culture? What expectations encourage students to share their mathematical thinking with others?

After you watch the clip, consider:

- Reflect on your teaching practices. How do you select problems for your students to solve?
- How can you make problem-solving lessons more meaningful to students in your classroom?

I often incorporate differentiation into growth problems by changing the number of stages in the pattern students are solving for. For example, when I pose the butterfly problem to my kindergarten students, I ask, "If one butterfly has two antennae, how many antennae do five butterflies have?" This question is appropriate for most of my students, although there are some students who need more of a challenge. For students needing more of a challenge, I increase the number of butterflies and also add the need to solve for the number of wings. Knowing your students and anticipating their needs will help you prepare recording sheets ahead of time that reflect higher or lower adjustments in numbers.

The following are two sets of strategies students have recorded in my classroom, and I've subsequently chosen to share them with the whole group during processing time.

> **TEACHING TIP: RUBRIC FOR SELECTING STUDENT WORK TO SHARE**
>
> Use the rubric on page 128 to help you select student work when scaffolding during processing time.

Set 1: Student Strategies

I started by sharing Thomas's work. Thomas's work is very clear; he made and labeled a set of nine circles to represent one cat. He numbered the remaining circles beginning with 10 for *"2 cats."* I showed Chantel's work next. Chantel used a familiar counting system (counting by fives) to solve this problem. She understands that five groups of nine is the same as nine groups of five. She used the commutative property of multiplication—this is powerful thinking! (See Figures 34, 35, and 36.)

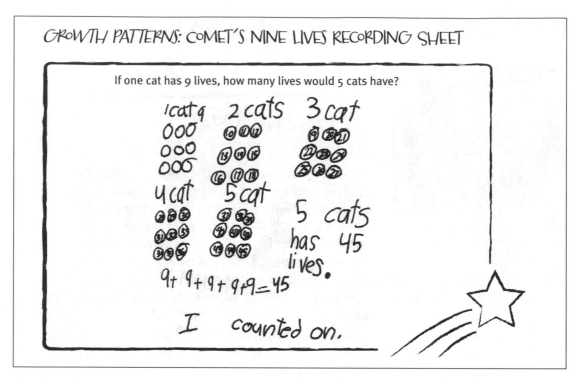

FIGURE 34 Thomas used five groups of nine to show his thinking in solving the *Growth Patterns* problem. He wrote, *"I counted on."* (See Thomas in 🎞️)

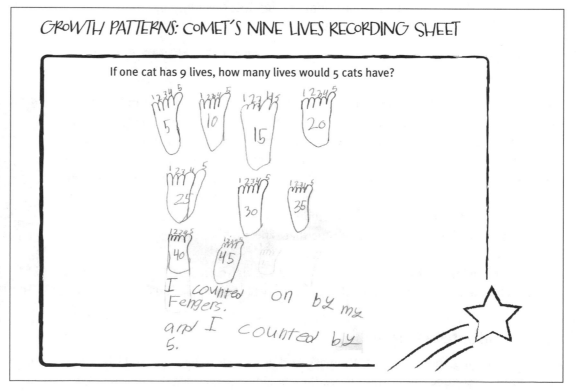

FIGURE 35 Chantel drew nine hands, labeled each hand's five fingers, then counted the fingers on the nine hands by fives and labeled this count.

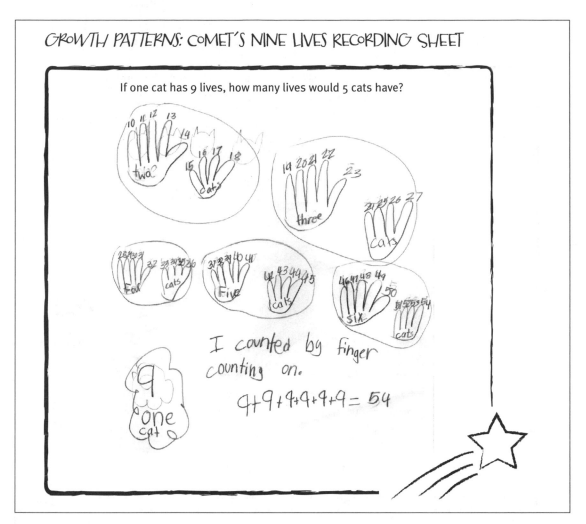

GROWTH PATTERNS: COMET'S NINE LIVES RECORDING SHEET

If one cat has 9 lives, how many lives would 5 cats have?

I counted by finger counting on.

9+9+9+9+9+9 = 54

FIGURE 36 Lorena solved the *Growth Patterns* problem for six cats rather than five cats, using her fingers to think this problem through. She made groups of nine fingers for each cat and wrote an equation showing repeated addition. (See Lorena in [CD icon])

Set 2: Student Strategies

The following pieces of student work were all done during the same problem-solving session; however, I changed the problem as needed to differentiate to meet my students' needs. During processing time, I started by sharing Joanna's work; she drew the five butterflies and counted all. Her work looks similar to many of the other students' work. I then shared the other two. Note that I gave Esteban and Jasmine each different problems to solve to meet their needs. (See Figures 37, 38, and 39.)

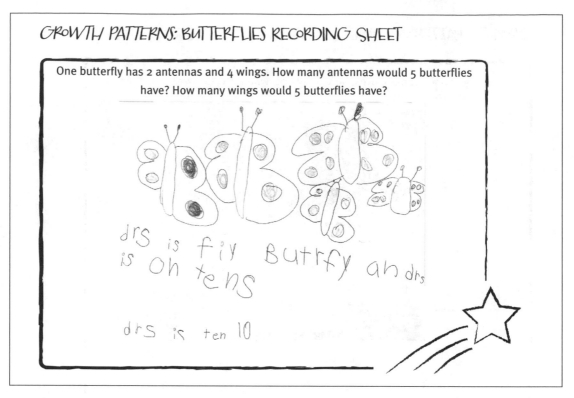

FIGURE 37 Joanna drew pictures and wrote, *"There is five butterfly and there is antennas there is ten"* to show her thinking in solving the problem.

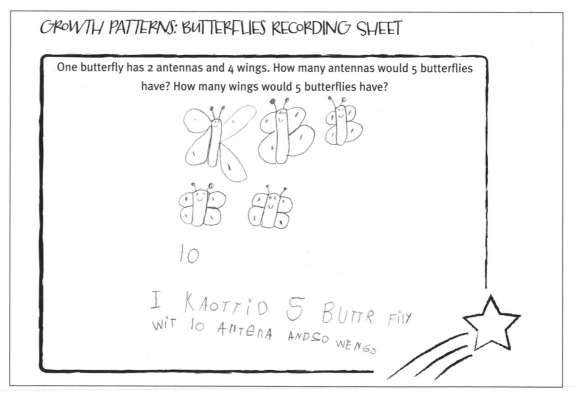

FIGURE 38 Esteban drew five butterflies in an organized manner and counted all the antennae and wings to solve this problem. He wrote, *"I counted 5 butterflies with 10 antennae and 20 wings."*

GROWTH PATTERNS: BUTTERFLIES RECORDING SHEET

One butterfly has 2 antennas and 4 wings. How many antennas would 5 butterflies have? How many wings would 5 butterflies have?

14 Antana AND

Γ Buttr Fliy

⊂8 WENGs

FIGURE 39 Jasmine drew butterflies in an organized manner and counted them all to find a solution for seven butterflies.

Formative Assessment in Action: Teacher and Student Checklists

For this lesson, use the Problem-Solving Teacher Checklist and the Problem-Solving Student Checklist on pages 137 and 138.

P-4 MY NAME IN COLOR TILES!

Related Lessons

Consider teaching first L-1 *Ten Black Dots* and L-4 *The Button Box*.

Overview

During this lesson, students use color tiles to create the letters in their first names. They then record their work using paper color tiles and graph paper. Their name "masterpieces" become the center of a mathematical task: writing equations that represent the combination of tiles in each letter. This lesson gives students many opportunities to explore composing and decomposing numbers. The personal nature of the lesson—students work with their own names—generates excitement and motivation.

Common Core State Standards

Aligned to the mathematical practices in the **Common Core State Standards**

Counting and Cardinality: Standard K.CC

> *Know number names and the count sequence.*
>
> *Count to tell the number of objects.*

Operations and Algebraic Thinking: Standard K.OA

> *Understand addition is putting together and adding to, and understand subtraction as taking apart and taking from.*

Operations and Algebraic Thinking: Standard 1.OA

> *Represent and solve problems involving addition and subtraction.*

Operations and Algebraic Thinking: Standard 2.OA

> *Represent and solve problems involving addition and subtraction.*

Goals for Student Understanding

These goals are aligned to the mathematical practices in the Common Core State Standards. Students will

- Make sense of problems and persevere in solving them.
- Reason abstractly and quantitatively.
- Construct viable arguments and critique the reasoning of others.
- Model with mathematics.
- Use appropriate tools strategically.

- Attend to precision.
- Look for and make use of structure.

Setting

Small group and individual

Time

Approximately one hour

Materials

color tiles
1-inch grid paper
1-inch paper color tiles (yellow, green, blue, and red)

large (12 by 18-inch) pieces of construction paper, 1 per student
glue sticks
My Name in Color Tiles! Teacher Checklist
My Name in Color Tiles! Student Checklist, 1 copy per student

Key Vocabulary

compose
decompose
equation
represent

> **TEACHING TIP: GLUE STICKS**
>
> Glue sticks are the easiest type of glue to use for this lesson, because students are working with small pieces of paper color tiles. Other types of glue (for example, white school glue) can be used when students are gluing their letters to large pieces of construction paper.

TEACHING DIRECTIONS

Part 1: Introducing the Lesson

1. Gather students in the whole-group area of your classroom. Remind students of experiences they have had with quick images and making arrangements of specific quantities (for example, L-1 *Ten Black Dots*). Tell students that they will make arrangements with color tiles. These arrangements will represent the letters in their first names.

2. Model making the first letter of your name with color tiles. To do this, touch the tiles whole side to whole side (not corner to corner). Then record the letter by gluing paper color tiles to a piece of grid paper. Show students how the grid paper makes it easier to line up the color tiles (it also is helpful at the recording stage of the lesson). Afterward, cut out the letter and lay it flat on a piece of construction paper. Explain to students that when all their letters are cut out, they will lay them on a piece of construction paper, leaving space between each letter. Then they will glue the letters to the paper to form their name!

Part 2: Creating Tile Letters

3. Have students work in small groups at tables. Assist students as necessary to think about how their letters should look. Some students may want all capital letters; others may want all their letters to be the same height. Make sure students understand that the color tiles must be assembled with a whole side touching a whole side (no corners to corners) to form the letters. This means that letters with curved lines are more difficult to make (but not impossible). Have conversations with students regarding this as it comes up.

> **TEACHING TIP: PAPER COLOR TILES**
>
> I use many paper color tiles throughout the school year. The tiles can be time-consuming to make. Consider asking parent volunteers and older students who volunteer to make these paper color tiles prior to the lesson.

> **TEACHING TIP: CONSTRUCTION PAPER**
>
> Start with one sheet of 12-by-18-inch paper for each student. Tape another sheet on as necessary to accommodate all the letters in a student's name.

4. After students have created the letters and mounted their names on pieces of construction paper, have them clean up the color tiles on their tables. The color tiles, especially in letter formations, take up a lot of table space; students will need this table space for the next step: recording.

Part 3: Recording Equations

5. Tell your students that they will now write equations. Each student will write an equation below each letter of his or her name. The equation will represent the letter. For example, Lorena's first letter is "L." Lorena used five tiles vertically placed and three horizontally placed to form her "L." This also forms the equation 5 + 3 = 8. Alternatively, students may create an equation based on the color of the tiles used. For example, if a student used 4 red tiles, 3 blue tiles, and 1 green tile for a letter in his or her name, he or she might write *4 + 3 + 1 = 8*. The student is decomposing the quantity of tiles that makes up each letter. Some students are willing to circle the manner in which they decompose the tiles in each letter; others do not want to write on their letters but will write the words to describe what they did when decomposing.

Part 4: Processing the Lesson

6. The processing piece to this lesson differs from other lessons described because all the students may not complete their name in one session. For those students who do finish in one session, have them share their color tile name. Have students reconvene in the whole-group area of your classroom. Hold each students' color tile name for everyone to see as the student explains how he or she decomposed each letter. If students need to be refocused while explaining, ask key questions such as the following:

Key Questions

- What did you record under this letter?
- Tell us why you wrote these numbers.
- How did you decide what to write under this letter?

As the teacher, and when selecting color tile names to share with the whole group, keep the following strategies in mind:

Strategies to Emphasize in My Name in Color Tiles!

- Uses numbers to represent how each letter was decomposed
- Writes to explain how each letter was decomposed
- Circles groups to show how tiles were grouped when decomposing
- Writes equations to show how each letter was decomposed

Extension

Color Tile Names: Last Names

For students who finish early and/or as a follow-up lesson, have students create their last names using the same directions presented earlier.

FORMATIVE ASSESSMENT IN ACTION: QUESTIONS

Use these questions to help guide your observations of students as they are engaged in the lesson. Your focused observations in turn support the instructional decisions you'll make for individual students and your class.

- How does the student create each color tile letter? Random colors? All one color? With a pattern?

- How does the student represent each letter? Letters with the same number of tiles? Letters all lowercase? Letters all capitals? Letters the same height?

- How does the student decompose tiles in each letter? By color? By arrangement?

- What does the student write to show how he or she decomposed tiles? Numbers? Equations? Words?

STUDENTS WHO STRUGGLE

Helping Students Who Need Support Writing

Some students may need support when writing the way they decomposed the tiles in the letters of their name. In this case I sit with each student and ask, "How can you group or clump the tiles in each letter? What can you write to show this on your paper?" Some students may write only numbers; some will write a number, then sound out the color word to write next to the number; and others will write equations.

Helping Students Who Are Not Writing Symbols Accurately

Although some students want to write equations, they usually are not writing the symbols accurately yet. I think of this as a time for *shared pen* or *interactive writing* in math. I encourage the student to write as much as possible, but if he or she needs support, I sit next to the student, plug in accurate symbols, and verbalize what I am doing.

WHAT HAPPENS IN MY CLASSROOM

MY NAME IN COLOR TILES!
VIDEO CLIP L

In this clip, the creative power of this lesson is brought to life; at the processing stage, kindergarteners Michael and Taya share how their name "masterpieces" became the center of a mathematical task (writing equations that represent the combination of tiles in each letter). First Michael shares the reasoning behind his color tile name, then Taya shares her thinking about her work. *As you watch the clip, consider:*

- What expectations are part of this classroom's culture? What expectations encourage students to share their mathematical thinking with others?

After you watch the clip, consider:

- Reflect on your teaching practices. How do you support students in strengthening their ability to communicate mathematically?

I usually teach this lesson in the spring. By this time, students have had many experiences explaining their thinking and are pretty articulate. The lesson can take some time; however, students love the context and are very motivated to create their names. It is a wonderful context to make connections to previous experiences children have had. Some students decompose based on color of tiles; others may decompose based on the shape of the letter. (See Figures 40 and 41.) Through sharing their color tile names, students motivate others to finish their names.

FIGURE 40 Cinthia wrote the equation *2 + 2 + 2 + 2 = 8* to represent the letter *i* in her name.

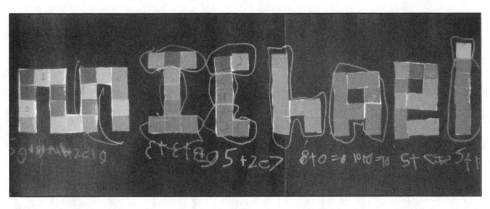

FIGURE 41 Michael wrote the equation *3 + 3 + 3 = 9* to represent the letter *i* in his name.

FORMATIVE ASSESSMENT IN ACTION:
TEACHER AND STUDENT CHECKLISTS

My Name in Color Tiles! Teacher Checklist

Checklists are invaluable in helping to focus your observations as well as to document student behaviors, responses, and reactions to lessons. Each column in the checklist specifies what to observe while students are engaged in the mathematical activity. Having the checklist ready on a clipboard, and easily accessible, helps to ensure necessary documentation and recording takes place. For more on using teacher checklists as a successful formative assessment practice, see page 15.

My Name in Color Tiles! Student Checklist

This checklist helps students monitor their own learning, set math goals, and ultimately share academic progress with their parents. Each child should have his or her own student checklist and should keep it in his or her student notebook. For more on using student checklists (including video clips) as a successful formative assessment practice, see page 20.

TEACHER CHECKLIST: MY NAME IN COLOR TILES!

Student Names and Date	Uses Random Color Tiles to Make Letters	Uses All One Color of Tiles to Make Letters	Uses a Color Pattern to Make Letters	Uses All Uppercase and All Lowercase; Uses a Combination	Decomposes by Color, Arrangement, Other	Writes Numbers, Numbers and Words, and/or Equations	Notes

STUDENT CHECKLIST

MY NAME IN Color TILES

NAME _____

	I made my name with paper color tiles!	I decomposed by color of tiles.	I decomposed by the shape of my letters.	I wrote numbers to explain how I grouped the tiles.	I wrote numbers and words to explain how I grouped the tiles.	I wrote equations to explain how I grouped the tiles.

DATE _____

DATE _____

DATE _____

DATE _____

P-5 THE FOUR-TRIANGLE PROBLEM

Related Lessons

Consider teaching first L-3 *Color Zoo*.

Overview

During this engaging lesson, adapted from *About Teaching Mathematics: A K–8 Resource, Third Edition* (Burns 2007), students put four triangles together to create a variety of polygons. They then convene as a whole group and post their shapes in polygon categories (the examination of the characteristics of shapes, the sorting, and clarification begins!). After students understand the procedures associated with this lesson, they absolutely love making geometric shapes. The lesson extends students' vocabulary, understanding of shapes, and understanding of how shapes can be put together to make new shapes. The lesson works fabulously for multilevel groups; students of all levels have access to building the shapes.

Common Core State Standards

Aligned to the mathematical practices in the **Common Core State Standards**

Geometry: Standard K.G

Identify and describe shapes (squares, circles, triangles, rectangles, hexagons, cubes, cones, cylinders, and spheres).

Analyze compare, create, and compose shapes.

Geometry: Standard 1.G

Reason with shapes and their attributes.

Geometry: Standard: 2.G

Reason with shapes and their attributes.

Goals for Student Understanding

These goals are aligned to the mathematical practices in the Common Core State Standards. Students will

• Make sense of problems and persevere in solving them.

• Reason abstractly and quantitatively.

• Construct viable arguments and critique the reasoning of others.

• Model with mathematics.

• Use appropriate tools strategically.

- Attend to precision.
- Look for and make use of structure.

Setting	Key Vocabulary
Whole group	corner
	edge
Time	hexagon
Approximately forty-five minutes	length
	parallelogram
Materials	pentagon
3-inch paper squares	polygons
scissors	quadrilateral
tape	rectangle
butcher paper	shape
glue stick	side
marker	square
The Four-Triangle Problem Teacher	trapezoid
Checklist	triangle
The Four-Triangle Problem Student	
Checklist, 1 copy per student	

TEACHING DIRECTIONS

Part 1: Introducing the Lesson

1. Gather students in the whole-group area of your classroom. Explain to students that they will be discovering how many different shapes can be made by putting four paper triangles together. There are two rules that need to be followed when putting the triangles together: (1) you can only put sides with the same length together and (2) you must use all four triangles.

2. Model and talk through the process of creating the paper triangles. First, each student will get two paper squares. Students will fold the squares on the diagonal and make a strong crease. They will then cut on this crease to form two triangles from each square.

3. From the two squares, you now have four triangles. Model lining up the sides, edge to edge, whole side touching a whole side. Remind students that (1) only sides of the same length can be placed together and (2) all four triangles must be used to create a new shape.

Part 2: Creating Shapes

4. Send students to work at their tables. Assist students as necessary. When students finish making a shape with their four triangles, have them tape the pieces together. Give them two more squares and ask them to make a different shape.

Part 3: Processing the Lesson

5. Hang a piece of butcher paper in a place students can easily see. After all your students have made a shape from their four triangles, gather the students in the whole-group area, shapes in hand.

6. First, explain to students that they have all made polygons—shapes with many sides (assuming that each student, when creating his or her shape, has lined up the sides of their four triangles, edge to edge, whole side touching a whole side). Write the word *Polygons* as a main heading (top and center) on the piece of butcher paper.

7. Now run your finger along each side of a shape and tell students this is a side. Ask students to count the sides on the shape they made. Ask if anyone made a shape with three sides. Tell students that shapes with three sides are called triangles. Write *Triangles* below the heading *Polygons*. Ask students who made triangles to come up and post their shape under the sub-heading *Triangles*. Students use tape or a glue stick to post their shapes. Assist as necessary.

8. Next write *Quadrilaterals* on the butcher paper. Explain to students that quadrilaterals are shapes with four sides. Ask students to say the word quadrilateral with you. Ask students to count the sides on their shapes. Did anyone make a quadrilateral? Possible quadrilaterals are a square, rectangle, trapezoid, and parallelogram. These can be listed below the word quadrilaterals on the paper; I only list the shapes that students have made.

9. Help students come up, sort, and post their quadrilaterals accordingly.

10. Next write *Pentagons* and tell students that pentagons have five sides. Ask students to count the sides of their shapes again. Has anyone made a shape with five sides?

11. Help students come up and post their pentagons accordingly.

12. Finally, write *Hexagons* on the butcher paper. Explain to students that hexagons have six sides.

13. Help students come up and post their hexagons accordingly.

14. Review the shapes listed on the butcher paper. Tell students that they will have time to revisit *The Four-Triangle Problem* to make shapes again.

Strategies to Emphasize in The Four-Triangle Problem

- Places sides of the same length together
- Uses all four triangles

Extension

Four Triangles Using Two Colors

This extension is most successful after students are very familiar with the lesson's procedures. It revisits *The Four-Triangle Problem* at a deeper level of understanding. You'll need 3-inch squares of two different colors. Give each student one square of each color. Ask students to use the two different-colored squares to create four triangles, then build a new shape. The use of two colors of paper allows students to see easily the shapes within the shape they create. During processing time, focus on which shapes can be put together to make a new shape—and the fact that there is more than one combination of shapes to make a new shape. Children are often excited to be able to see, visually—thanks to the use of the two colors—how the same shape can be built in a variety of ways how and it can be used to build a variety of more shapes!

Repeated Experiences

Although this lesson is introduced as a whole-group experience, offer it as a repeated experience in independent center work. Students can work individually or with a partner to continue creating shapes. This also gives them a chance to discover how to make shapes they may not have found—but were introduced to—during the whole-group processing time of the lesson.

FORMATIVE ASSESSMENT IN ACTION: QUESTIONS

Use these questions to help guide your observations of students as they are engaged in the lesson. Your focused observations in turn support the instructional decisions you'll make for individual students and your class.

- Does the student explore many different possibilities before taping or does he or she tape the first shape together that he or she makes?

- Does the student make several shapes or one shape?

- Does the student work alone or does he or she discuss ideas with others at the table?

- What vocabulary does the student use throughout this activity?

- Is the student able to count and keep track of the number of sides on the shape that he or she creates?

STUDENTS WHO STRUGGLE

Sometimes a student may have difficulty determining which sides are the same length. I help these students by modeling. I place two of the triangles' sides next to each other with the same length to show him or her how the sides match. I emphasize to the student that this how it will look when the sides are the same length. For this activity we can only tape the sides together if the lengths are equal or the same. The sides have to match.

WHAT HAPPENS IN MY CLASSROOM

Students are surprised when they discover that the six-sided shape, an irregular hexagon, does not resemble the regular hexagon they are so familiar with from their work with pattern blocks, yet both are hexagons. The pentagons and hexagons that are made from four triangles are irregular shapes. Repeating *The Four-Triangle Problem* allows you to reinforce important vocabulary and build understandings of geometric concepts.

FORMATIVE ASSESSMENT IN ACTION: TEACHER AND STUDENT CHECKLISTS

The Four-Triangle Problem Teacher Checklist

Checklists are invaluable in helping to focus your observations as well as to document student behaviors, responses, and reactions to lessons. Each column in the checklist specifies what to observe while students are engaged in the mathematical activity. Having the checklist ready on a clipboard, and easily accessible, helps to ensure necessary documentation and recording takes place. For more on using teacher checklists as a successful formative assessment practice, see page 15.

The Four-Triangle Problem Student Checklist

This checklist helps students monitor their own learning, set math goals, and ultimately share academic progress with their parents. Each child should have his or her own student checklist and should keep it in his or her student notebook. For more on using student checklists (including video clips) as a successful formative assessment practice, see page 20.

Teacher Checklist: The Four-Triangle Problem

Student Names and Date	Explores Possibilities, Then Tapes Shape	Tapes Shape Immediately	Creates More Than One Shape, Which Shapes?	Works Alone or with Others	Counts Number of Sides on Shape	Vocabulary Used	Notes

STUDENT CHECKLIST

NAME _____

THE FOUR-TRIANGLE PROBLEM

I made shapes using four triangles!	I counted and kept track of the number of sides on my shape.

DATE _____

DATE _____

DATE _____

DATE _____

P-6 STUDENTS WRITE THE CONTEXT

Related Lessons

Consider teaching first all the previous problem-solving lessons.

Overview

During this lesson, students take ownership over the context as they write the story to an equation. The lesson incorporates writing with math and provides insight to students' creative thinking. What experiences do students bring to write a problem for this equation? What connections do they make to create a mathematical situation for an equation? Afterward, students use strategies that make sense to them to solve the problem and write to explain their mathematical thinking. This lesson gives the teacher insight into students' fluency with mathematical strategies and models that they use for representation. After the problem is solved, processing time allows opportunities to scaffold and share students' work.

Common Core State Standards

Operations and Algebraic Thinking: Standard 2.OA

Represent and solve problems involving addition and subtraction.

Use place value understanding and properties of operations to add and subtract.

Aligned to the mathematical practices in the **Common Core State Standards**

Goals for Student Understanding

These goals are aligned to the mathematical practices in the Common Core State Standards. Students will

- Make sense of problems and persevere in solving them.

- Reason abstractly and quantitatively.

- Construct viable arguments and critique the reasoning of others.

- Model with mathematics.

- Use appropriate tools strategically.

- Attend to precision.

- Look for and express regularity in repeated reasoning.

Setting

Whole group

Time

Approximately forty-five minutes

Materials

a variety of counters
mathematical tools (hundred chart, open
    number line, and so forth)

Reproducible R: *Students Write the Context*
    Recording Sheet, 1 copy per student
Students Write the Context Teacher
    Checklist
Students Write the Context Student
    Checklist, 1 copy per student

Key Vocabulary

communicate
model
represent
strategy

TEACHING DIRECTIONS

Follow the same directions as stated in P-1 *How Many Frogs?*, except first tell students you would like them to write a story to go along with the equation. Give every student a copy of Reproducible R: *Students Write the Context* Recording Sheet. Students first write the story problem, then solve the equation. When selecting student work to share during processing time, keep the following strategies in mind.

Strategies to Emphasize for Students Write the Context

- Writes a story that makes sense with the equation

- Uses multiple strategies that make sense

- Uses mathematical tools

FORMATIVE ASSESSMENT IN ACTION: QUESTIONS

Use these questions to help guide your observations of students as they are engaged in the lesson. Your focused observations in turn support the instructional decisions you'll make for individual students and your class.

- Does the student understand the task?

- Does the student's story make sense with the numbers in the equation?

- Does the student's story problem stand out with the six traits of writing in mind? (The six traits are ideas, organization, voice, sentence fluency, word choice, and conventions.)

- Does the student solve the problem in more than one way?

- How does the student represent his or her mathematical thinking? Counters (physical model), pictures, words, numbers, hundreds chart, open number line, strips and singles?

- Is the student able to communicate his or her ideas to others? Which setting is he or she able to share in? Individually, small group, or whole group?

STUDENTS WHO STRUGGLE

If a student has difficulty expressing himself or herself in writing, encourage this student to do his or her personal best to write their ideas using words and pictures. After the student finishes writing, ask the student to read what they wrote to you. Take dictation of what the student reads to you to refer back to when necessary.

> **TEACHING TIP: RUBRIC FOR SELECTING STUDENT WORK TO SHARE**
>
> Use the rubric on page 128 to help you select student work when scaffolding during processing time.

WHAT HAPPENS IN MY CLASSROOM

STUDENTS WRITE THE CONTEXT
VIDEO CLIP M

In this clip, second-graders collaborate on the three parts of a problem-solving lesson (introducing, solving, and processing) as applied to a *Students Write the Context* lesson for the equation 53 – 27. *As you watch the clip, consider:*

- How does having students share their problem-solving strategies strengthen each person's mathematical understandings?

- How are students supported as they develop their skills in communicating mathematical thinking to one another?

After you watch the clip, consider:

- How can you make manipulatives more accessible to students in problem-solving settings?

- Reflect on your teaching practices. When and how do you decide which of your students will share their problem-solving strategies?

During processing time, after a strategy to represent mathematical thinking is shared, such as drawing pictures, I say to the whole group, "Raise your hand if you used pictures to solve the problem." I repeat this process for each strategy shared. I do not ask each child to come up to talk about his or her work, but I do validate useful strategies and recognize all students who are using them. The following are some of the strategies students have recorded in my classroom. I asked students to share work in the order presented here during our processing time. (See Figures 42 through 44.)

> *See Clip K Growth Patterns to hear Dana give a narrative overview of the problem-solving process.*

Student Strategies

STUDENTS WRITE THE CONTEXT RECORDING SHEET

Write a story problem for 32 – 17 =

Hope had 32 balls, she gave Jasmine 17 balls, How manny dos Hope have now. Show your work.

Solve the problem using pictures, words, numbers, and mathematical tools that make sense to you.

5+2+10=17
15 20 22 32

I Stard at 32 and –10 and how I got 22 – 2 = 20 and – 5 = 15 my user is 15

FIGURE 42 Emily wrote a story problem about Hope giving Jasmine 17 of her 32 balls; she showed her thinking with drawing and an open number line.

STUDENTS WRITE THE CONTEXT RECORDING SHEET

Write a story problem for 32 – 17 =

Mya had 32 puppy's she gave 17 puppy's to her best friend Tara how many puppy's does Mya have now?

Solve the problem using pictures, words, numbers, and mathematical tools that make sense to you.

32–17=15

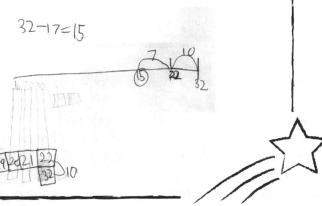

FIGURE 43 Tara wrote a story problem about Mya giving her best friend 17 of her 32 puppies; she demonstrated her thinking with two mathematical models, an open number line and the relevant part of the hundreds chart.

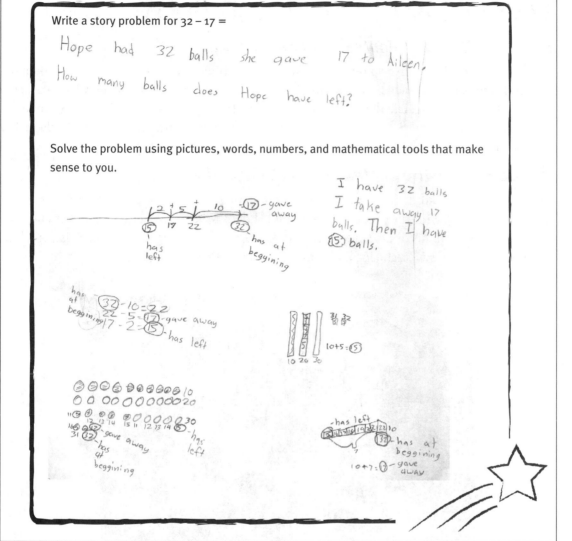

STUDENTS WRITE THE CONTEXT RECORDING SHEET

Write a story problem for 32 – 17 =

Hope had 32 balls she gave 17 to Aileen.
How many balls does Hope have left?

Solve the problem using pictures, words, numbers, and mathematical tools that make sense to you.

I have 32 balls
I take away 17
balls. Then I have
15 balls.

FIGURE 44 Jasmine wrote a story problem about Hope giving 17 of her 32 balls to Aileen; she showed her mathematical fluency by representing many ways to solve the problem, including an open number line, strips and singles, a drawing with labels, and the relevant part of the hundreds chart.

FORMATIVE ASSESSMENT IN ACTION: TEACHER AND STUDENT CHECKLISTS

Students Write the Context Teacher Checklist

Checklists are invaluable in helping to focus your observations as well as to document student behaviors, responses, and reactions to lessons. Each column in the checklist specifies what to observe while students are engaged in the mathematical activity. Having the checklist ready on a clipboard, and easily accessible, helps to ensure necessary documentation and recording takes place. For more on using teacher checklists as a successful formative assessment practice, see page 15.

Students Write the Context Student Checklist

This checklist helps students monitor their own learning, set math goals, and ultimately share academic progress with their parents. Each child should have his or her own student checklist and should keep it in his or her student notebook. For more on using student checklists (including video clips) as a successful formative assessment practice, see page 20.

TEACHER CHECKLIST: STUDENTS WRITE THE CONTEXT

Student Names and Date	Writes an Appropriate Context for the Equation	Uses Organization (Drawings, Numbers Are Lined Up)	Multiple Representations (Pictures, Words, Numbers, Physical Model, Strips and Singles).	Uses Mathematical Tools (Hundreds Chart, Open Number Line).	Shares Work During Processing Time	Notes

STUDENT CHECKLIST

NAME _____

STUDENTS WRITE THE CONTEXT

I wrote a story that makes sense with the equation provided.	I was organized.	I used multiple representations to solve the problem (pictures, words, numbers, manipulatives, strips and singles).	I used mathematical tools (hundreds chart, open number line, strips and singles).	I shared my thinking during processing time.

DATE _____

DATE _____

DATE _____

DATE _____

REPRODUCIBLES

Reproducible A: Teacher Checklist Template

Reproducible B: Student Checklist Template

Reproducible C: Parent Questionnaire

Reproducible D: My Math Goal Is . . .

Reproducible E: Note to Parents

Reproducible F: Shake and Spill *Recording Sheet*

Reproducible G: Pattern Dance

Reproducible H: Number Cards 1–10

Reproducible I: +1, –1 Cards

Reproducible J: Quick-Image Cards

Reproducible K: The Button Box *Recording Sheet*

Reproducible L: Lottie's New Beach Towel *Recording Sheet, Versions 1 and 2*

Reproducible M: How Many Frogs? *Recording Sheet, Versions 1 and 2*

Reproducible N: Combinations of Ants *Recording Sheet*

Reproducible O: Combinations of Grapes *Recording Sheet*

Reproducible P: Growth Patterns: *Comet's Nine Lives Recording Sheet*

Reproducible Q: Growth Patterns: *Butterflies Recording Sheet*

Reproducible R: Students Write the Context *Recording Sheet*

Reproducible S: Five Little Speckled Frogs *Picture Cards*

Reproducible T: Student Checklist: Number Recognition 0–20*

Reproducible U: Student Checklist: I Can Count! 1–30*

Reproducible V: Student Checklist: I Can Count! 1–50*

*All reproducibles are also available as downloadable, printable versions at
www.mathsolutions.com/howtoassessreproducibles*

*Available online only

TEACHER CHECKLIST TEMPLATE

Reproducible A

Student Names and Date							Notes

STUDENT CHECKLIST TEMPLATE

NAME

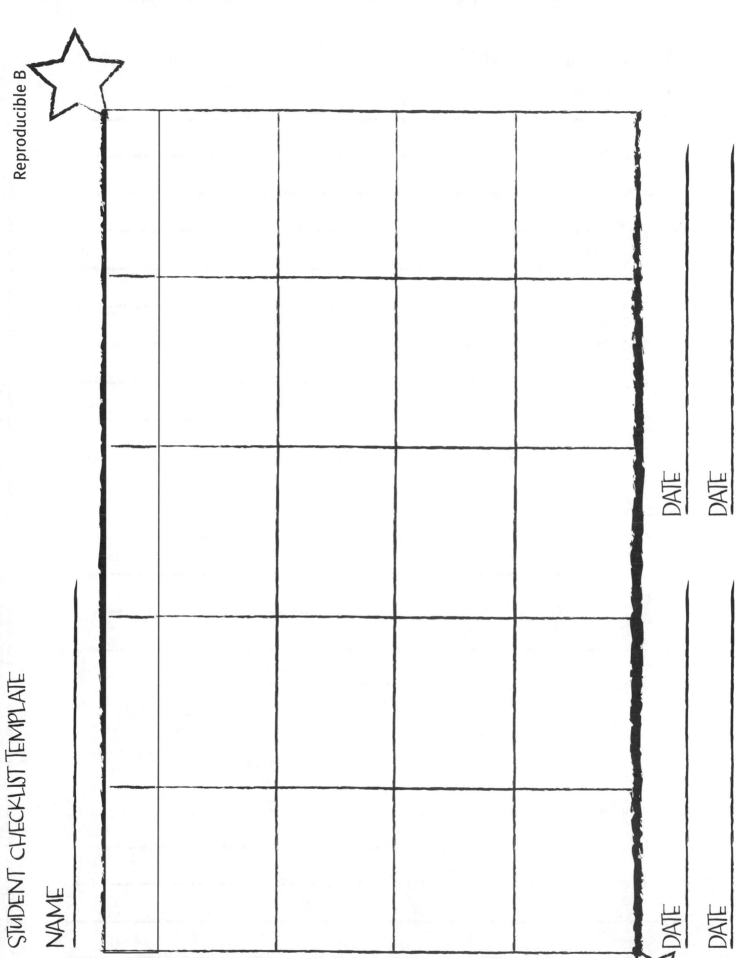

DATE

DATE

DATE

DATE

PARENT QUESTIONNAIRE

Personal Information

Student's Name: _____

Student's Birthday: _____

Parent's Name: _____

Home Address: _____

Phone Number: (hm) (cell) (wk) _____

What is the best time to reach you? _____

Emergency Phone Number: _____

Who can pick your child up from school? _____

Who is not allowed to pick your child up from school? _____

_____

Child/Family History

What are the names of the family members living with you? _____

_____

What does your child like to do as a family? _____

_____

At what ages were the following milestones for your child?

☐ Crawling

☐ Talking

☐ Walking

☐ Potty training

Were there any complications during childbirth? _____

Did your child go to preschool? Describe his or her experiences. _____

_____

_____

Does your child watch TV? How many minutes/hours per day? ⎯⎯⎯⎯⎯⎯⎯⎯⎯⎯

Do you read to your child? List his or her favorite books. ⎯⎯⎯⎯⎯⎯⎯⎯⎯⎯

⎯⎯⎯⎯⎯⎯⎯⎯⎯⎯

What time does your child go to bed? ⎯⎯⎯⎯⎯⎯⎯⎯⎯⎯

Describe your child in one word. ⎯⎯⎯⎯⎯⎯⎯⎯⎯⎯

Home–School Communication

We send a newsletter to keep you informed of relevant information. We also send homework packets that will help reinforce skills that have been taught.

⎯⎯⎯⎯⎯⎯⎯⎯⎯⎯

How much time could you set aside to help your child with homework? ⎯⎯⎯⎯⎯⎯⎯⎯⎯⎯

Have you designated a specific time and place that your child can do homework? ⎯⎯⎯⎯⎯⎯⎯⎯⎯⎯

Parents as Volunteers

In what areas would you like to volunteer?

☐ In the classroom

☐ On fieldtrips

☐ Making classroom materials at home

☐ Providing refreshments for special events

☐ Assisting in special areas (cooking, sewing, sharing a special talent, and so on)

Teacher Expectations

Would you be interested in attending a parent meeting that offered ideas to help your child with reading, writing, and math?

⎯⎯⎯⎯⎯⎯⎯⎯⎯⎯

What would be the best time for you to attend a parent meeting? During the day or during the evening?

⎯⎯⎯⎯⎯⎯⎯⎯⎯⎯

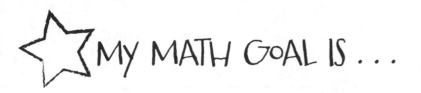 MY MATH GOAL IS . . .

Reproducible D

NAME _____   DATE _____

MY MATH GOAL IS . . .

_____

_____

TEACHER NOTES:

 From *How to Assess While You Teach Math: Formative Assessment Practices and Lessons, Grades K–2: A Multimedia Professional Learning Resource* by Dana Islas. © 2011 Scholastic Inc. Permission granted to photocopy for nonprofit use in a classroom or similar place dedicated to face-to-face educational instruction. Downloadable at www.mathsolutions.com/howtoassessreproducibles.

WE ARE SETTING GOALS!

I am excited to send a copy of the math goal your child has set. Your child and I talked about how this goal can be met. Please talk to your child about his or her goal and help him or her work toward achieving it!

- ☐ Read over your child's goals.
- ☐ Make a plan with your child.
- ☐ Sign and return this form.
- ☐ Celebrate your child's accomplishments.

STUDENT'S NAME: _____

PARENT'S COMMENTS: _____

_____

_____

PARENT'S SIGNATURE: _____

SHAKE AND SPILL RECORDING SHEET

Reproducible F

NAME _____

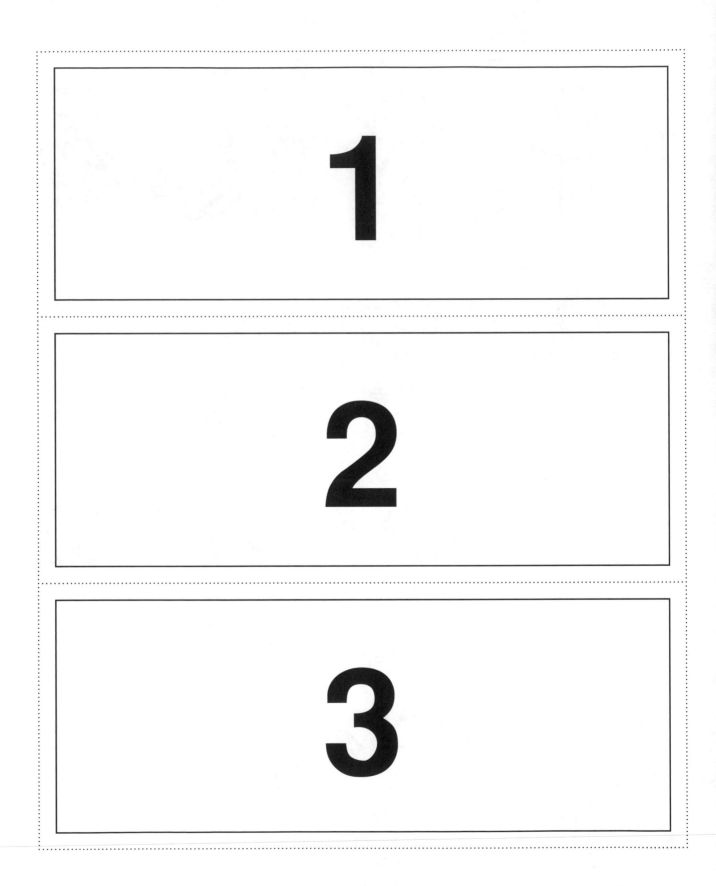

4

5

6

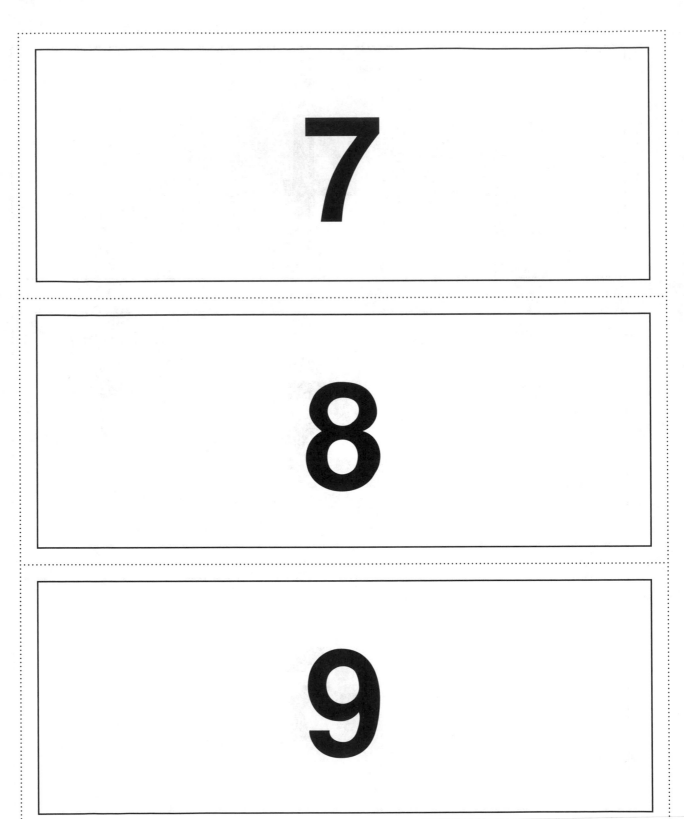

7

8

9

10

+1	**−1**
+1	**−1**
+1	**−1**
+1	**−1**
+1	**−1**

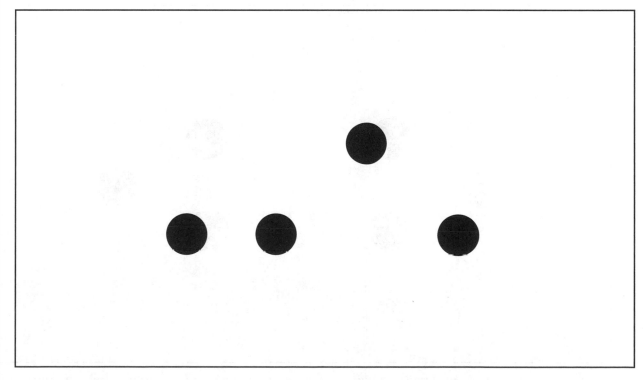

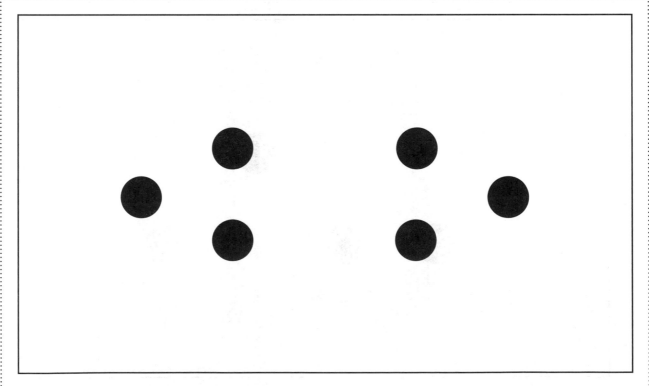

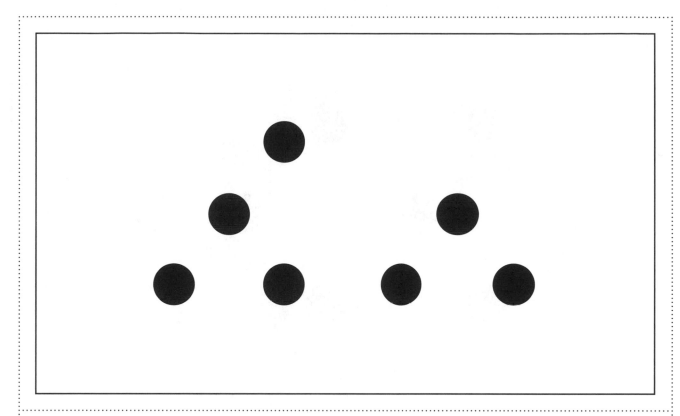

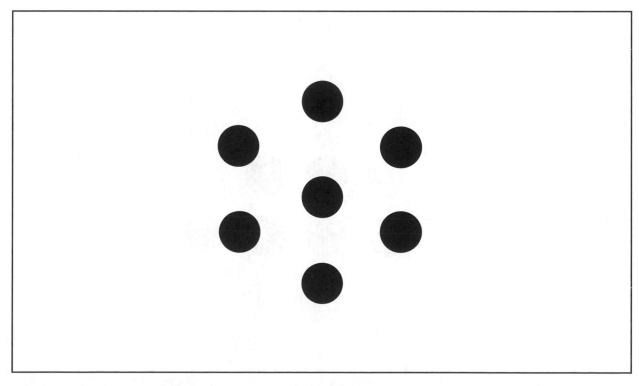

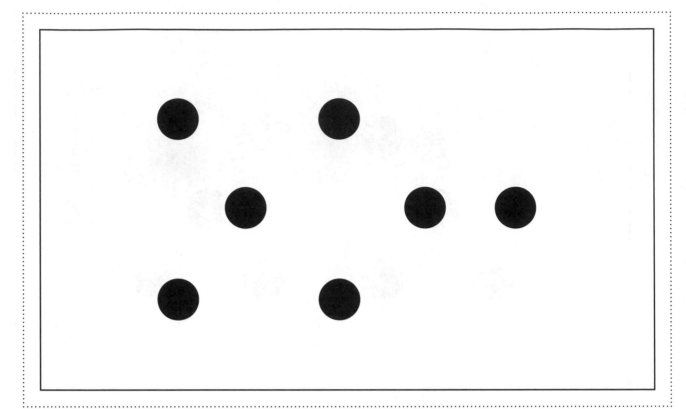

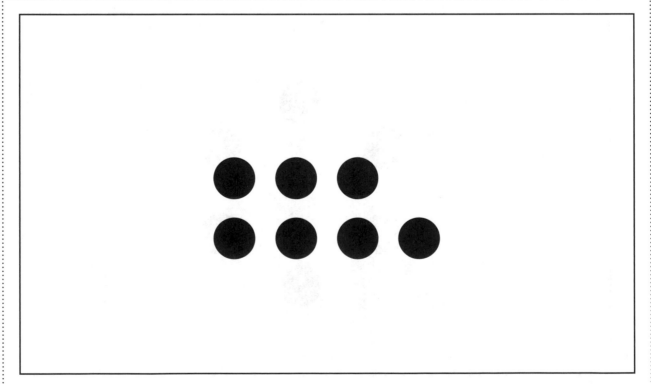

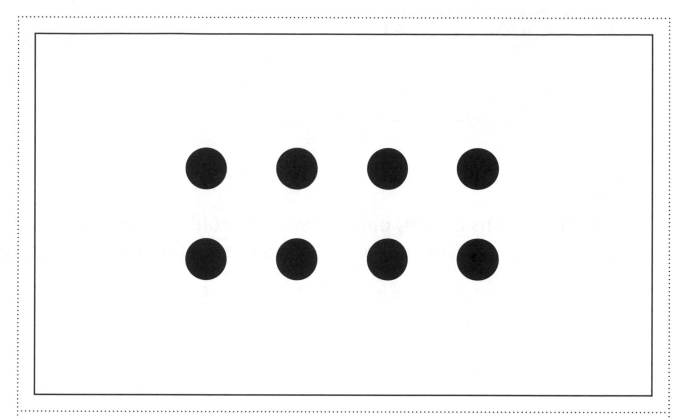

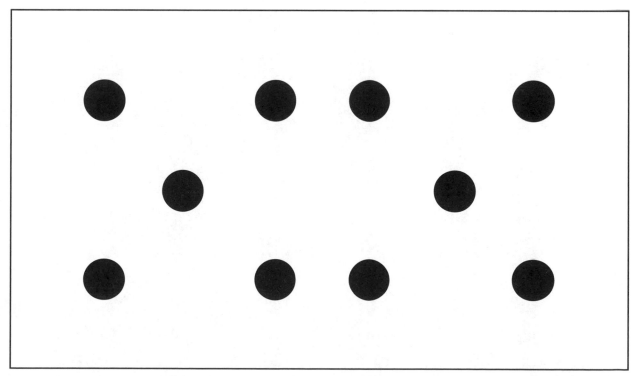

 THE BUTTON BOX
RECORDING SHEET

NAME _____

Buttons

Sort your buttons in many different ways. Record the way you sorted the buttons by using pictures, words, and number sentences (equations).

LOTTIE'S NEW BEACH TOWEL
RECORDING SHEET, VERSION I

NAME _____

Lottie and Herbie found seashells at the beach. During the day Herbie lost 2 of the shells. They had 6 seashells when they went home. How many shells did they find?

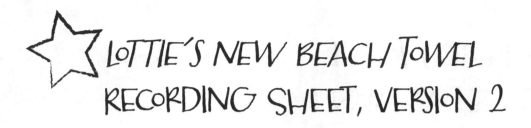

LOTTIE'S NEW BEACH TOWEL
RECORDING SHEET, VERSION 2

NAME _____

Lottie and Herbie found 8 seashells while they were at the beach. Herbie lost 2 of the seashells. How many seashells does Lottie still have?

NAME _____

Frogs

Five speckled frogs sat on a hollow log. Two jumped into the water. How many frogs are still on the hollow log?

HOW MANY FROGS?
RECORDING SHEET: VERSION 2

NAME _____

Frogs

Seven speckled frogs sat on a hollow log. Some jumped into the pool.
Now there are 4 speckled frogs on the log. How many jumped into the
pool?

COMBINATIONS oF ANTS RECORDING SHEET

NAME _____

The Ants

Gizelle and Benjamin were digging in the sand. While they were digging they found 6 ants. Some of the ants were red; some of the ants were black. How many ants could be red? How many ants could be black?

NAME

The Grapes

Thomas and Ana had 10 grapes to share. Some of the grapes were green; some of the grapes were purple. How many grapes could be green? How many could be purple?

GROWTH PATTERNS: COMET'S NINE LIVES RECORDING SHEET

NAME _____

Comet's Nine Lives

If one cat has 9 lives, how many lives would 5 cats have?

NAME _____

Butterflies

One butterfly has 2 antennas and 4 wings. How many antennas would 5 butterflies have? How many wings would 5 butterflies have?

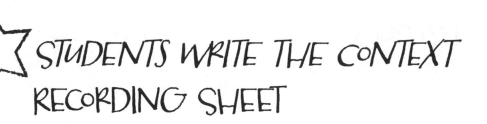

STUDENTS WRITE THE CONTEXT
RECORDING SHEET

NAME _____

Write a story problem for 32 – 17 =

Solve the problem using pictures, words, numbers, and mathematical tools that make sense to you.

FIVE LITTLE SPECKLED FROGS
PICTURE CARDS

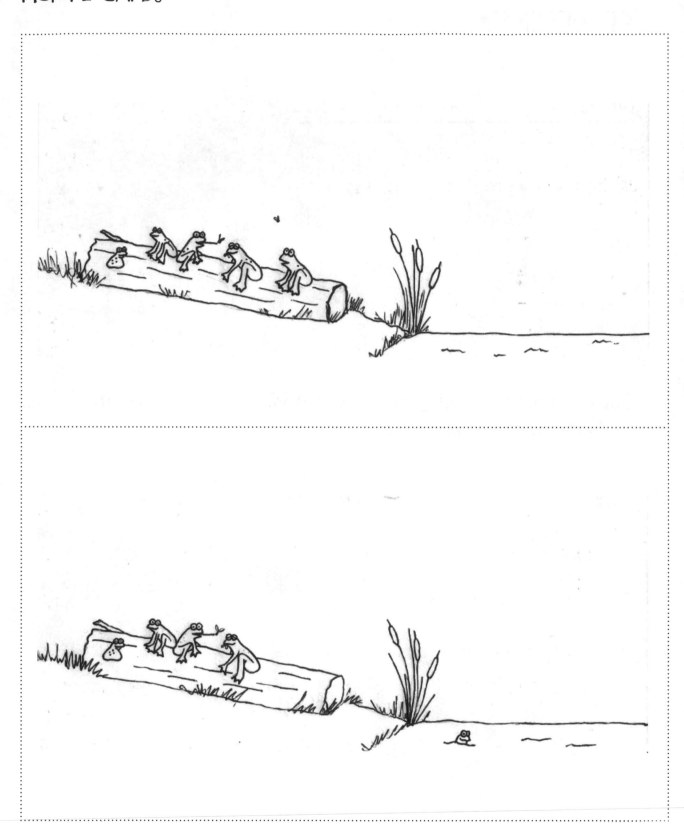

FIVE LITTLE SPECKLED FROGS
PICTURE CARDS

(continued)

FIVE LITTLE SPECKLED FROGS
PICTURE CARDS
(continued)

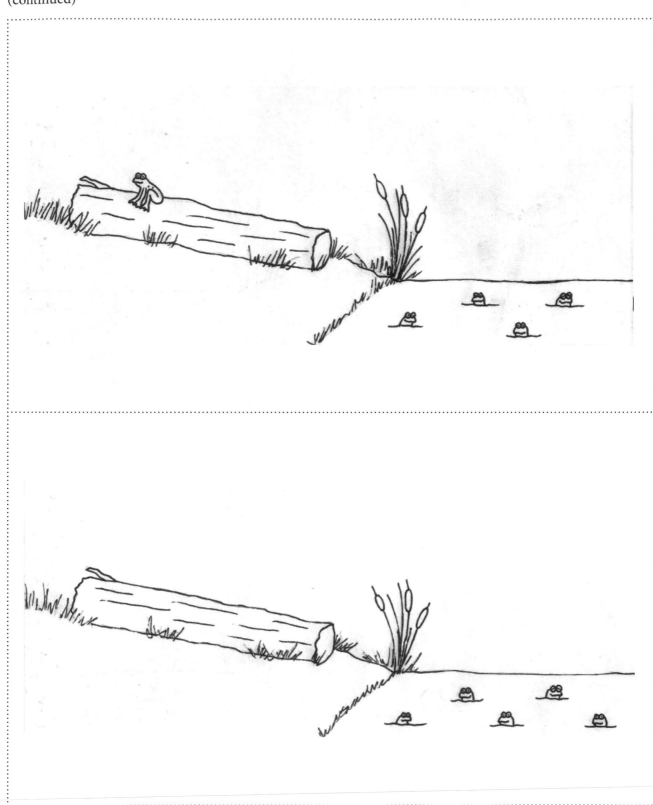

REFERENCES

PROFESSIONAL RESOURCES

Arizona Daily Star. 2010. "Award-Winning Teacher Speaks to Best in Education." January 9. http://azstarnet.com/news/opinion/editorial/article_2217ecf7-5ebb-52ac-9115-a4a19d90721d.html.

Bresser, Rusty, Kathy Melanese, and Christine Sphar. 2008. *Supporting English Language Learners in Math Class, Grades K–2*. Sausalito, CA: Math Solutions.

Burns, Marilyn. 2007. *About Teaching Mathematics: A K–8 Resource, Third Edition*. Sausalito, CA: Math Solutions.

Conklin, Melissa. 2010. *It Makes Sense! Using Ten-Frames to Build Number Sense, Grades K–2*. Sausalito, CA: Math Solutions.

Covey, Stephen. 2004. *7 Habits of Highly Effective People*. New York: Free Press.

_____. 2008. *The Leader in Me: How Schools and Parents Around the World Are Inspiring Greatness, One Child at a Time*. New York: Free Press

Parrish, Sherry. 2010. *Number Talks: Helping Children Build Mental Math and Computation Strategies, Grades K–5: A Multimedia Professional Learning Resource*. Sausalito, CA: Math Solutions.

Richardson, Kathy. 2003. *Assessing Math Concepts: Hiding Assessment*. Bellingham, WA: Mathematical Perspectives.

CHILDREN'S LITERATURE

Baker, Keith. 1995. *Hide and Snake*. San Diego, CA: Voyager Books.

_____. 2004. *Quack and Count*. San Diego, CA: Voyager Books.

Brett, Jan. 2001. *Comet's Nine Lives*. New York: Puffin Books

Carle, Eric. 1990. *The Very Quiet Cricket*. New York: Philomel Books

Christelow, Eileen. 2006. *Five Little Monkeys*. New York: Clarion Books.

Crews, Donald. 1986. *Ten Black Dots*. New York: Mulberry Books.

Ehlert, Lois. 1989. *Color Zoo*. New York: HarperCollins.

_____. 2000. *Cuckoo*. San Diego, CA: Voyager Books.

Jenkins, Emily. 2005. *Five Creatures*. New York: Frances Foster Books.

Jonas, Ann. 1995. *Splash!* New York: Greenwillow Books.

Ling, Mary. 2007. *See How They Grow: Butterflies*. New York: DK.

Mathers, Petra. 2001. *Lottie's New Beach Towel*. New York: Aladdin Paperbacks.

Morozumi, Atsuko. 1993. *One Gorilla: A Counting Book*. New York: Farrar, Straus and Giroux.

Reid, Margarette S. 1990. *The Button Box*. New York: Puffin Books.

Smith, Nikki. 2006. *Five Little Speckled Frogs*. Nikki Smith Books.

Walsh, Ellen Stoll. 2009. *Mouse Count*. San Diego, CA: Voyager Books.

Williams, Sue. 1988. *Let's Go Visiting*. San Diego, CA: Voyager Books.

Wood, Audrey. 2004. *Ten Little Fish*. New York: Blue Sky Press.

DATE DUE

PRINTED IN U.S.A.